CW01090758

New

Sky

3

Students' Book

Brian Abbs
Ingrid Freebairn
David Bolton

Contents

1 They're making a film.

1 🎧 02 Listen and read

Jake and Rose Spencer are in London for the day. They meet an Australian boy and girl, Ollie Ford and his sister, Jess.

Jake: Hey look! There's a boy and a girl at the top of that building!

Ollie: What's happening?

Jake: They're making a film – an Alex Rider film. I read about it in the paper.

Ollie: Oh, right. A spy film! Cool!

Rose: I like your accent. Are you Australian?

Ollie: Yes, we're from Melbourne. But we're living in London right now, near the City Airport.

Jess: Dad works for an airline company. Where do you live?

Rose: We live in East London too.

Ollie: Great! Look! There's Alex Pettyfer. He plays Alex Rider in the film.

Rose: Quick! He's leaving. Excuse me, Alex! Can I have your autograph, please?

Now listen and repeat.

2 Check

Correct the sentences.

1 Ollie and Jess are ~~English~~. *Australian*
2 They're from Sydney.
3 Ollie has got a London accent.
4 His dad works for a film company.
5 Jake and Rose live in West London.
6 Jess asks Alex Pettyfer for his autograph.

Everyday phrases

- Look!
- What's happening?
- Oh, right.
- Quick!
- Excuse me!

Look and learn

Remember!

The present
Remember and complete.

Present simple

Positive
I/We _live_ in East London.
He/She ... in Melbourne.

Negative
I/We ... live in Manchester.
He/She ... live in Sydney.

Questions
Where ... you live?
Where ... your dad work?

> Check out the Grammar Store on page 95

Present continuous

Positive
I'm/They're _making_ a film.
He/She ... talking to a film star.

Negative
I ... /They ... making a TV programme.
He/She ... talking to me.

Questions
What ... he doing?
Where ... you living right now?

3 Read and write

Read and complete the magazine article.

Star profile: Keira Knightley

Keira Knightley is a British film star. She's from West London. Her mum and her dad are both actors. She is famous for her parts in Hollywood films like _Pirates of the Caribbean_ and British films like _Bend it like Beckham_ and _Atonement_.

Keira [1] ... (work) very hard - she usually [2] ... (make) three or four films a year. But right now she [3] ... (have) a holiday. She [4] ... (not stay) in a hotel in Hollywood. She [5] ... (live) in her own house in Central London for a month.

Keira [6] ... (love) football and when she's in England she often [7] ... (go) to watch her favourite team, West Ham. 'It's great in London. It's my home. I just [8] ... (go) to Los Angeles to work. What about the future? I [9] ... (not know). I'm young. I never [10] ... (think) about the future. I [11] ... (enjoy) my life at the moment.'

4 Listen

The new friends continue talking. Listen and complete the information about Ollie Ford.

Name: _Ollie Ford_
Nationality: _Australian_
Age: ...
School: ...
Home town: ...
Favourite sport: ...
Favourite food: ...

5 English in action: Personal information

You meet an Australian student. Act the conversation, using the prompts.

• What/your name? _What's your name?_
• Where/come from?
• What/doing here?
• Where/staying?
• Where/go to school?
• What sports/play?
• Want/have a hamburger?

6 Memory check: Places in town

Say which two places these people want to go to.

1 'I want to park my car, then catch a train.'
   a car park + the station
2 'We want to have dinner, then go dancing.'
3 'I want to have a coffee, then buy a new CD.'
4 'We want to change some money, then buy food.'
5 'I want to buy a book, then buy some stamps.'
6 'We want to catch a bus, then see a film.'

7 Write

Write a newspaper article about a famous film or pop star from your country. Use these questions to help you.

• What is he/she famous for?
• Is he/she married?
• Where does he/she live?
• What is he/she doing at the moment?
• What does he/she do in his/her free time?

Portfolio

2   I like this one.

1 🎧 (1/04) Listen and read

Mum: We're going to buy a new cycle helmet for Rose.

Dad: All right. Let's meet at four o'clock. Don't be late.

Mum: OK. See you!

Rose: Jake, I like this one.

Jake: Which one?

Rose: The red one with the black stripes on it. Look.

Ranu: What about that one?

Rose: Yes, that's nice too.

Jake: Hang on, Ranu! Look at those trainers!

Ranu: Which ones?

Jake: The black ones.

Rose: Don't be silly, Jake! You've got three pairs of trainers already.

Mum: Hurry up, you two! We're meeting Dad at four.

Rose: Excuse me, how much is this helmet?

Man: It's £14.99.

Rose: OK. Can I have it, please?

Man: Sure. Here you are. And here's your change!

Rose: Thanks! What am I going to buy with 1p?

Now listen and repeat.

Everyday phrases

- All right.
- Don't be late.
- Hang on!
- Don't be silly.
- Hurry up [you two].
- How much [is this helmet]?
- Sure.

2 Check

Right (✓), wrong (✗) or don't know (DK)?

1   Rose wants a new cycle helmet. ✓
2   She wants a black helmet with red stripes.
3   Ranu sees a nice helmet.
4   Jake is looking at trainers.
5   Rose's got two pairs of trainers.
6   Rose's mum buys the helmet for her.

3 🎧 Memory check: Money

Say these prices. Then listen and check.

a) 99p   b) 50p   c) £1   d) £3   e) £5.50   f) £37.95

> ### Look and learn
>
> **Which one(s) (do you like)?**
>
> | (I like) | the blue one(s). |
> | | the big one(s). |
> | | the one with the red stripes on it. |
> | | the one(s) with black stripes. |

4 English in action: Shopping

a) Look at the pictures. Complete the conversation with *one/ones* and the price.

A: *Excuse me. How much are the sunglasses?*
B: *Which ...?*
A: *The green ... .*
B: *They're ... .*
A: *OK, can I have them, please?*
B: *Sure, here you are.*
A: *Thanks.*

b) One of you is a customer, the other is a shop assistant. Look at the pictures and buy the things.

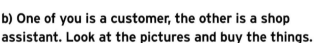

> ### Look and learn   *Remember!*
>
> **The future**
> **Remember and complete.**
>
> ***Going to* future for plans and intentions**
>
> | Positive | Negative |
> |---|---|
> | I'm *going to* buy a helmet. | I'm ... to buy trainers. |
>
> **Questions**
> What ... you ... buy?
>
> **Present continuous for future arrangements**
>
> | Positive | Negative |
> |---|---|
> | I'm *meeting* Dad at half past three. | I'm ... Dad at four o'clock. |
>
> **Questions**
> When ... you meeting Dad?

5 Speak

a) Talk about your plans and intentions.

1   **A:** *What are you going to do this evening?*
    B: *I'm going to watch the football match on TV.*

1   What/do/this evening?
2   Where/go/next Saturday?
3   What/do/next month?

b) Talk about your future arrangements.

1   **A:** *Who are you meeting after school today?*
    B: *I'm meeting my friend Mariella.*

1   Who/meet/after school today?
2   Where/go/tomorrow?
3   What/do/at the weekend?

6 🎧 Listen

Listen to Rose talking to her friend Lisa. Complete the sentences.

1   Lisa's *going to do* her homework after school.
2   Then ... a film on TV.
3   Rose's new Australian friends ... to her house.
4   They ... at six o'clock.
5   Then they ... a computer game.
6   Lisa ... her History project before she goes to Rose's house.

7 🎧 Song: *Dedicated Follower of Fashion* by The Kinks

Go to page 92 and listen and join in the song.

3 What did you do?

To: Sam
Cc:
Subject: Weekend

Hi Sam!

We had a great weekend. How was yours? What did you do? We went to the Bluewater Shopping Centre. It was fun. We took our new Australian friends, Ollie and Jess. We met them about two weeks ago. Anyway, I went to the games shop and I made a big mistake – I bought the latest Xbox game with my birthday money. I started to play it when I arrived home and it was rubbish. Ollie left his mobile in the games shop and when we went back to look for it, we found it! He was lucky.

Oh, I nearly forgot. Guess what happened when we first met Ollie and Jess? We saw Alex Pettyfer, the actor from *Stormbreaker*! He came and talked to Rose. She wanted his autograph but she didn't have her autograph book. He said 'That's OK' and gave her a signed photo. I thought that was nice of him. Then he wrote 'Stormbreaker lives!' on her arm. Mum took this photo of it. Rose didn't wash for a week!

Please write back soon.

Cheers,

Jake

P.S. Thanks very much for the CD! It was great.

1 🎧 Read

Jake is writing an email to his friend Sam. Read the email.

Then listen and repeat the second paragraph.

2 Check

Who do you think said this? Complete the chart.

	Alex	Ollie	Rose	Jake	Mum
1 'I've got a new game but it's rubbish.'				✓	
2 'Oh, no! Where's my mobile phone?'					
3 'Can I have your autograph, please?'					
4 'Yes, sure, but where's your autograph book?'					
5 'I'm going to take a photo of your arm.'					
6 'I'm not going to wash for a week!'					

Everyday phrases

- It was fun/rubbish.
- I nearly forgot.
- Guess what [happened] …
- Please write back soon.
- Thanks very much for the [CD].

Look and learn

Past simple
Remember and complete.

Positive
Alex *talked* to Rose yesterday
We ... to Alex yesterday.

Negative
He ... talk to me.
We ... talk to him.

Questions
Where ... they see him?

Note! a few days **ago**   a week **ago**   two months **ago**

---

3 🎧 Write and listen

a) Find the past simple forms of these verbs in Jake's email. Then write them in the correct column.

• do • have • be • go • take • meet • make
• buy • start • arrive • leave • find • forget
• happen • see • come • talk • want • say
• give • think • write

Regular verbs	Irregular verbs
start *started*	*do* *did*

b) Now listen and repeat.

4 Read and write

Complete the article with the past simple of the verbs.

Cash surprise

A funny thing ¹*happened* to 16-year-old student Lucy Sanders last Monday. She ²... (want) £10 so she ³... (go) to the cash machine at her bank. She ⁴... (take) £10 from the machine and ⁵... (start) to walk away. Then the machine ⁶... (give) her another £10, and then another and then another. Ten minutes later she ⁷... (have) £1000! So what did Lucy do? She went into the bank, ⁸... (talk) to the manager and gave him the £1000. He ⁹... (be) very surprised. 'Lucy was very honest,' he ¹⁰... (say) yesterday. One of Lucy's friends said she was crazy but everyone else said she ¹¹... (do) the right thing!

5 Speak

Ask and answer questions about Jake's email.

1 **A:** *Where did Jake and Rose go at the weekend?*
   B: *They went to a shopping centre.*

1 Where/Jake and Rose/go at the weekend?
   They/to a shopping centre.
2 Who/they/take? They/Ollie and Jess.
3 What/Jake/buy? He/a computer game.
4 What/Ollie/leave in the shop? He/his mobile.
5 Which actor/they see? They/Alex Pettyfer.
6 What/he/give Rose? He/a photo.

6 Memory check: Free time

List free time activities.

At home	In town	Sports
listen to music	*go shopping*	*play basketball*

7 Speak

a) Ask your friends what they did in their free time. Ask about the times in the box.

• yesterday evening   • on Friday night
• last weekend   • a month ago   • last summer

A: *What did you do yesterday evening?*
B: *I went swimming.*

b) Tell the class.

Anton watched a DVD yesterday evening. Hanna ... .

8 Write

Write an email to a friend. Tell him/her about something funny or strange that happened to you. Use Jake's email in Exercise 1 to help you. Portfolio

9 🎧 Limerick

Go to page 94 and listen and complete the limerick.

London

1 🎧 Listen and read

～A trip on the River Thames～

There are interesting things to see on both sides of the river and around every bend.

1 There are the Houses of Parliament. They have 1,100 rooms and five kilometres of corridors! There's also Big Ben, which isn't the name of the famous clock but the bell inside the tower.

2 Then there's the London Eye. It's 135 metres high and the views from the top are fantastic.

3 King William I built the Tower of London in 1078. It was a palace and a prison. Now it's a museum.

4 Tower Bridge looks old but it's one of London's newest bridges. They finished it in 1894. When the bottom part of the bridge goes up, you can still walk across the top.

5 At Greenwich there are famous old ships and a line on the ground which marks 0° longitude. There you can stand with one foot in the eastern hemisphere and the other in the western hemisphere.

London:
Amazing facts and figures

- About 8 million people live in London. 30% were not born in the UK.

- The British Library has over 150 million books.

- There are 24 universities and colleges in London with 350,000 students.

- There are 33 bridges over the River Thames and 4 tunnels under it.

- Big Ben is the biggest clock in the UK. Its diameter is 7.5 metres. The hour hand is 2.7 metres long.

- 46,500 people run in the London Marathon every year.

- 27 million people visit London every year. It's the world's most popular tourist destination.

ear Greenwich is Canary Wharf. ears ago there were docks there. oday there are thousands of modern ffices, apartments and shops.

New words

- side • bend • bell • tower • palace • prisoner • mark (v)
- eastern • hemisphere • western • docks • offices • apartment
- instead • tunnel • diameter • marathon • destination

2 Quiz

How much can you remember? Match the questions and answers.

1 g)

1	How many rooms are there in the Houses of Parliament?	a) 1894
2	How high is the London Eye?	b) 150 million
3	When did they build the Tower of London?	c) 8 million
4	When did they finish building Tower Bridge?	d) 135 metres
5	How many people live in London?	e) 27 million
6	How many books has the British Library got?	f) 46,500
7	How many bridges over the Thames are there in London?	g) 1,100
8	How many people run in the London Marathon?	h) 33
9	How many people visit London every year?	i) 1078

3 Listen

Listen and say where the people are.

1 *They're at Tower Bridge.*   2 ...   3 ...   4 ...

4 Speak

In groups, talk about London and agree on the three most interesting things about the city.

A: *I think it's really interesting that ...*
B: *Yes, but I think it's amazing that ...*

Project

 Portfolio

A holiday postcard

Writing tip

How to end a letter or postcard.

I must go.	Say hi to ... .
Give my regards/love to	See you soon/next week.

Imagine you are on a week's holiday in London. Write a postcard to a friend. Answer the questions as you write.

- Are you enjoying your holiday?
- When did you arrive?
- What did you do or see yesterday?
- What are you going to see tomorrow?

Hi Tom

I'm enjoying my holiday in London. I ...

Revision

1 A Spanish boy is talking to a Swedish boy in London. Correct their mistakes.

Luis: 1 ~~Where do you stay?~~
Where are you staying?

Hans: 2 I stay in a hotel near here.
3 I visit England with my family.

Luis: 4 You like London?

Hans: 5 Yes, I like. Why are you here?

Luis: 6 I learn English.

Hans: 7 But you are speaking good English.

Luis: 8 No, I not. I make a lot of mistakes!

2 🎧 Sounds fun /ŋ/

Listen, then listen and repeat.

Cycling, playing, running, walking.
We're having fun.
And we never stop talking!

3 Do the sums and find the total price.

1 b)

1 [**65p**] + [**£1.15**]
2 [**£1.20**] + [**75p**]
3 [**£1.99**] + [**10p**]
4 [**55p**] + [**£1.50**]

a) Two pounds five pence
b) One pound eighty
c) One pound ninety-five
d) Two pounds nine pence

4 Rewrite the conversation. Change the underlined word to *one* or *ones*.

Sean: 1 I want some new trainers. These <u>trainers</u> are old.
I want some new trainers. These ones are old.

Beth: 2 Which <u>trainers</u> do you like?

Sean: 3 I like those <u>trainers</u> in the window.

Beth: 4 I like that T-shirt. The red <u>T-shirt</u>.

Sean: 5 The <u>T-shirt</u> with the A on the front?

Beth: 6 Yes, that <u>T-shirt</u>.

5 Complete the conversation using these words and phrases.

• Can • one • Excuse me • Here • Which • It's

A: 1 *Excuse* me. How much is that scarf?
B: 2 ... one?
A: The blue and green 3 ... .
B: 4 ... £13.99.
A: OK. 5 ... I have it, please?
B: Sure. 6 ... you are.
A: Thanks.

6 Complete the sentences with one verb in the present continuous and the other verb in the *going to* future.

1 Sam's _coming_. (come) to my house at six o'clock.
   We'_re going to play_ (play) my new computer game.
2 We' ... (leave) at three o'clock. We ... (play) tennis.
3 Mum ... (take) me to the Bluewater Shopping Centre tomorrow.
   I ... (buy) some new trainers.
4 My Australian cousin ... (arrive) tomorrow. He ... (work) for an English company in London.
5 **A:** When ... you ... (do) your homework?
   B: I can't do it now. I ... (meet) Matt in five minutes.

7 Complete the missing forms of the verbs.

Present	Past	Present	Past
1 *have*	had	6 say	...
2 leave	...	7 ...	gave
3 ...	saw	8 buy	...
4 take	...	9 ...	did
5 ...	went	10 find	...

8 Complete this page from Jake's diary with the past simple forms of the verbs.

SATURDAY 24th JULY

My cousin Jason ¹_arrived_ (arrive) from America on Saturday. We ²... (meet) him at London airport and then ³... (take) him to our house. He ⁴... (talk) all the time! But he ⁵... (have) a really cool American accent. My mum ⁶... (make) a big pizza. He ⁷... (say) it ⁸... (be) better than the pizzas back home in America. And then he ⁹... (wash) the dirty dishes – he was very surprised we ¹⁰... (not have) a dishwasher! Before he ¹¹... (leave) the next day, he ¹²... (give) me a real American baseball cap!

9 Where are these people? Choose from:

• a music shop • a café • a cinema • a restaurant • a station • a bank • a post office • a book shop

1 'Can we have two tickets for the new James Bond film, please?' _a cinema_
2 'Have you got the latest Justin Timberlake CD?'
3 'Can I have a coffee, please – an espresso?'
4 'Can I change these euros into pounds, please?'
5 'What time does the next train to London leave?'
6 'Have you got an English dictionary, please?'
7 'Can we have two pizzas, please?'
8 'I want to send this letter to Poland, please.'

10 Chat time

a) You meet a boy/girl for the first time. In pairs, write a conversation. Then act it out.

A: *Where do you live?*
B: *I live in London.*

Student A	Student B
Ask where Student B lives.	
	Say where you live.
Ask what Student B does in his/her free time.	Say what you do in your free time.
Ask what Student B did last summer.	
	Say what you did.
Ask Student B what he/she is going to do tomorrow.	Say what you're going to do tomorrow.
Ask Student B what he/she wants to do on Saturday.	Say what you're doing on Saturday morning. Say you're free in the afternoon.

b) Listen to Jake and Ollie and compare your conversation.

What can you do?

I can:

- ask and talk about personal information ☐
- say what is happening ☐
- ask and talk about plans, intentions and future arrangements ☐
- ask and talk about things that happened in the past ☐

6 He couldn't speak.

The wild boy

In 1797, in southern France, some hunters found a strange boy in the woods. He was about nine and was completely wild. They took him back to the village and he lived with a local woman. While he was with her, he escaped twice and ran back to the woods. In June 1800, he finally came out of the woods himself.

Nobody could find out anything about the boy because he couldn't speak or understand French. They called him Victor. Victor ate strange food: he didn't eat fruit or vegetables, he ate leaves and plants. Of course, he could climb trees easily and was happiest in the woods.

When he was about fourteen, he met Doctor Gaspard Itard. The doctor wanted to study the wild boy and tried to teach him to speak. After some years, Victor could understand quite a lot of French. He could also read simple words but he couldn't say more than two words. One of them was *lait* (milk).

Victor died in Paris in 1828 at the age of forty. In 1970, the French film director, Francois Truffaut, made a famous film about Victor's life called *L'Enfant Sauvage* (The Wild Boy).

1 Read

Read the article. Then listen and repeat the first two paragraphs.

2 Check

Match the two parts of the sentences.

1	In 1797 some hunters	a) strange food.
2	He was	b) at the age of 40.
3	He ate	c) him some French.
4	Doctor Itard taught	d) found a strange boy.
5	Victor died	e) completely wild.

3 Memory check: Verbs of action

Find twelve verbs of action in the wordsnake. Then listen and check.

1 talk

talkreaduseswimskateboardspellplaypaintwalkwriterideltell

Look and learn

Modal: *could/couldn't* (ability)

Positive	**Negative**
He **could** climb trees.	He **couldn't** speak.
They **could** speak French.	They **couldn't** teach him French.

Questions
What **could** he say?

***Yes/No* questions**
Could he say many words?
Yes, he **could.**/No, he **couldn't**.

Think about language
Is *could* the same or different with *I*, *you*, *he*, *she*, *it*, *we* and *they*?

14

4 Speak

Ask a friend about the things he/she could or couldn't do when he/she was five. Use the verbs in Exercise 3. Tell the class.

A: *Could you ride a bike when you were five?*
B: *No, I couldn't.*
A: *Could you swim?*
B: *Yes, I could.*

Writing tip

Linkers: *when* and *after*

When you are writing about the past, you can link ideas with *when* and *after*.

- **When** they found him, he couldn't speak a word.
- **After** some years, he could understand quite a lot.

Find another sentence with *when* in the text in Exercise 1.

---

5 Write

Use the information below to write about a very clever boy, Toby Harcourt.

Could = ✓   Couldn't = ✗

Age		
1	walk ✓	talk ✗
2	climb the stairs ✗	run ✓
3	read ✗	write his name ✓
4	use a computer ✓	swim ✗
5	ride a bike ✗	tell the time ✓

When he was only one, Toby could walk but he couldn't talk. When he was two, he couldn't climb the stairs but he could run.

6 🎧 Listen and read

Complete the conversation with *could* or *couldn't* and the verbs. Then listen and check.

Miki: Can I talk to you?

Ania: Yes, of course.

Miki: For me English is very difficult. How much English ¹*could you speak* (you/speak) when you first came to this school?

Ania: I ²... (read) a bit of English - a short story in a newspaper for example. And I ³... (say) 'Hello' and 'Thanks.' But I ⁴... (speak) English very well.

Miki: What was your biggest problem?

Ania: I ⁵... (understand) when people spoke to me. They spoke so fast! Of course, I ⁶... (answer) simple questions like 'What's your name?'. But I ⁷... (answer) more difficult questions because I ⁸... (understand) them. Some people in London have very strange accents!

Miki: I agree!

7 We were getting bored.

1 New words: Prepositions of motion

Listen and repeat. Then match the prepositions and pictures.

- into • past • through
- across • over • out of
- around • along • under

1 across

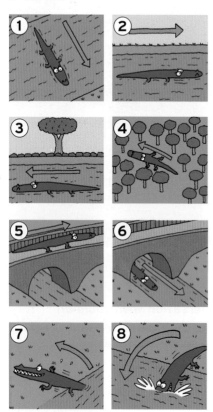

2 Read

Read the article about a forest fire.

British teens in dramatic fire escape

Matt Duncan reports from Toulon

Four young British teenagers were celebrating in the south of France last night after they helped their friends to escape from a forest fire. 'We didn't do very much really,' said Kylie Roberts, 13, from Portsmouth. 'We were just lucky.'

Kylie and her friends were on a school trip at a campsite near a seaside town. While they were staying there, the weather got hotter and hotter.

'It was very hot and we were getting a bit bored,' said Kylie, 'so we decided to get up really early, when it was still cool, and go for a bike ride.'

The four friends were cycling along a road through some woods when suddenly they saw black smoke over the hills behind their campsite. 'It was a really big fire!' said Kylie. 'It was coming across the forests and the fields – and it was moving in the direction of our campsite!'

Fortunately for her friends and all the campers, Kylie had her mobile phone with her. She called the campsite and gave the alarm. The campers all managed to get out of the camp before the fire arrived. French fire fighters then used planes and helicopters to drop water and sand on the fire. Eventually the fire went out.

'When I phoned home, my mum was watching TV and we were on the evening news so we were famous for five minutes!' said Kylie.

Now listen and repeat the first and second paragraphs of the article.

3 Check

Number the events in the correct order.

a) Kylie phoned the campsite. `3`
b) Kylie and her friends went for a bike ride. `1`
c) The fire went out. `5`
d) Kylie phoned her mother. `6`
e) The campers left the campsite. `4`
f) Kylie and her friends saw black smoke. `2`

4 Write

Write where the man went in pictures 1-9. Use the words in the box.

- bridge (x2)   • river (x3)   • cottage   • wood
- field   • house

First he went through a wood. Then he went past a house. After that he went …

  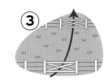

 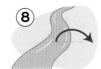 

Look and learn

Past continuous

Positive
I/He/She **was staying** on a campsite.
You/We/They **were cycling** along a road.

Negative
I/He/She **wasn't staying** in a hotel.
You/We/They **weren't walking** along a road.

Questions
What **were** they **doing**?

Yes/No questions
Were they **walking**?
Yes, they **were**./No, they **weren't**.

With *when* and *while*
She was watching TV **when** Kylie phoned.
While she was watching TV, Kylie phoned.

Think about language
When or *while*?
We use *when/while* before the past simple.
We use *when/while* before the past continuous.

5 Speak

In pairs, ask and say what you were doing at these times.

A: *What were you doing at 6 o'clock this morning?*
B: *I was sleeping.*

- 6 o'clock this morning
- 8.30 this morning
- 3 o'clock yesterday afternoon
- 7 o'clock yesterday evening
- 3 o'clock last Saturday afternoon
- 9 o'clock last Sunday morning.

6 Speak

In pairs, ask and say what the people at the campsite were doing when they heard the alarm.

A: *What was Peter doing?*
B: *He was sleeping.*

Peter

Mr and Mrs White

Serge

Paolo and Roberto

Tony

Nicole

7 Write

Write what the people were doing. Make two sentences using *when* and *while*.

a) *Peter was sleeping when he heard the alarm.*
b) *While Peter was sleeping, he heard the alarm.*

8 Limerick

Go to page 94 and listen and complete the limerick.

1 Listen and read

Jake and Rose are visiting Ollie and Jess.

Ollie: Do you want to see my saxophone? Here it is.

Jake: Wow! Can you play it? Are you any good?

Ollie: I'm not bad. I'm in the school orchestra.

Jake: My mum used to play the sax.

Ollie: Cool. Did she use to play a lot?

Jake: Not really. But she was quite good, I think.

Ollie: Does she still play?

Jake: No, not any more.

Jess: Come on, Rose. Let's do some karaoke. There's a good James Blunt song here.

Rose: Oh no. I'm hopeless at singing.

Jess: I didn't use to be any good when I first did karaoke. So don't worry!

Rose: OK but you hold the mike.

Jess: Right. Here goes. 'You're beautiful ...'

Ollie: Jess, must you? You sound like a sick goat.

Rose: Ollie, don't be so mean to your sister!

Now listen and repeat.

Everyday phrases

- Not really.
- ... not any more
- Come on, [Rose].
- You sound like [a sick goat].
- [I'm] hopeless.
- Here goes.
- [Jess], must you?
- [Ollie], don't be so mean [to your sister].

2 Check

Right (✓), wrong (✗) or don't know (DK)?

1 Ollie plays in an orchestra. ✓
2 Jake's mum played the saxophone.
3 She plays it now.
4 Jess is good at singing.
5 Jess holds the mike.
6 The boys sing with the girls.

3 New words: Musical instruments

a) Listen and repeat. Then match. Which four instruments are not in the pictures?

- piano • recorder • saxophone
- trumpet • drums • violin • keyboards
- electric guitar • acoustic guitar • flute
- trombone • harmonica • accordion

1 electric guitar

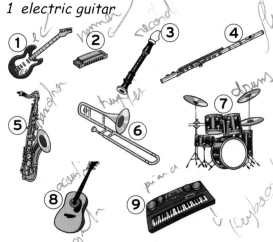

b) Name four instruments used in an orchestra and four in a rock band.

4 🎧 Listen

Listen and write the instrument each member of the band plays.

1 Carl: *the violin* 2 Tom: ... 3 Ned: ...
4 Cassie: ... 5 Diana: ...

> ### Look and learn
>
> **Modal: *used to***
> **Positive**
> She **used to** play the sax.
>
> **Negative**
> She **didn't use to** play a lot.
>
> **Question**
> What instrument **did you use to** play?
>
> ***Yes/No questions***
> Did he **use to** play the drums?
> Yes, he **did**./No, he **didn't**.

5 Speak

a) Work in pairs. A is an American TV reporter, B is David and Victoria Beckham's son, Brooklyn.

1 **A:** *Which teams did your dad use to play for?*
 B: *He used to play for Manchester United and Real Madrid.*

1 **A:** Which teams/your dad/play for?
 B: he/Manchester United and Real Madrid
2 **A:** Which team/he/play for now?
 B: he/play/LA Galaxy
3 **A:** What/your mum/be?
 B: she/pop singer
4 **A:** What/do/now?
 B: she/design/clothes
5 **A:** Where/you/live?
 B: We/London and Madrid
6 **A:** Where/you/live now?
 B: We/Los Angeles

b) Talk about David or Victoria Beckham's life before and now.

David Beckham used to play for Manchester United but now he ... .
Victoria Beckham used to be a pop singer but now she ... .

6 Speak

Talk about your own appearance and habits.

I used to have blonde curly hair but I've got straight brown hair now.

7 Read

Read about Jake's grandad, Harry, who used to be a professional footballer.

❝This is a photo of me forty years ago. I used to play for a team called Bristol City. In those days footballers didn't use to earn much money. I didn't have my own house. I used to live with my parents. And I used to drive a small family car, not an expensive sports car. What sort of clothes did I use to wear? I can't really remember, but I think I used to wear ordinary clothes, not expensive designer clothes like footballers do today.
  But I enjoyed it. People used to ask for my autograph. I was famous! I remember I used to have very long hair – it was the fashion in those days.❞

8 Check

Complete the questions and then answer them.

1 What/Harry/use to/be?
 What did Harry use to be? He used to be a professional footballer.
2 Which team/use to/play for?
3 He/use to/earn much money?
4 Where/he/use to/live?
5 What kind of car/use to/drive?
6 What/people/use to/ask him for?

9 Write

Write an email to an English friend about one of your parents or grandparents when they were at school. Write about:

- what he/she used to do
- where he/she used to live
- the clothes he/she used to wear
- who he/she used to live with
- how much pocket money he/she used to earn

9  Across the curriculum
The solar system

1 🎧 **Read**

Pythagoras
(582-497BC)

Eratosthenes
(276-196BC)

Ptolemy
(120-180AD)

Copernicus
(1473-1543)

Galileo
(1564-1642)

What did people first believe?

Thousands of years ago everyone used to believe the earth was flat. They thought it was like an island with water all around it. Above it was a dome – the sky. The sun and the stars moved across this dome.

What did the ancient Greeks believe?

The ancient Greeks had other ideas. Pythagoras (582-497BC) thought that the earth wasn't flat. It was round and the earth, the moon and the stars moved around the sun. Another Greek, Eratosthenes (276-196BC), calculated that the circumference of the earth was 40,000 km, which was almost exactly right.

How did Ptolemy change this idea?

About 400 years later another Greek, Ptolemy (120-180AD), changed everything. He wrote that the earth, and not the sun, was at the centre of the universe and that the moon, the sun and the stars moved around the earth. For the next 1,400 years most people in Europe used to believe this.

What did Copernicus and Galileo believe?

In the 16th century a Polish mathematician and astronomer Nicolas Copernicus (1473-1543) went back to the ideas of the ancient Greeks. He said that the sun, not the earth, is at the centre of our solar system. Copernicus's ideas were not popular at the time. In 1609 the Italian astronomer Galileo (1564-1642) watched the movement of the stars with the first telescope. He could see that the sun was at the centre of our solar system so he proved that Copernicus was right.

New words

- everyone • believe • flat • island • dome
- moved • ancient • calculated • circumference
- change • universe • mathematician
- astronomer • solar system • watched
- movement • telescope

2 Check

Answer the questions.

1 Where was Pythagoras from?
2 Who first measured the earth's circumference?
3 Why were the ideas of Pythagoras and Ptolemy so different?
4 Where was Copernicus from?
5 How did Galileo prove the theories of Copernicus?

3 Listen

Listen and complete this description of the life of Copernicus.

The life of Nicolas Copernicus

Nicolas Copernicus was born in [1] *1473* in Torun, Poland. Both his parents died before he was [2] … and Nicholas went to live with his [3] … . He studied Mathematics at Krakow University then Law and Medicine in Italy.

He finished his [4] … page book about the movement of the stars in [5] … but it was not published until [6] … . A friend gave him the first copy of his book on the day he died. Archeologists found his grave and skull in [7] … in Frombork Cathedral.

Martin Luther wrote of Copernicus, 'This fool wants to turn the entire science of [8] … upside down.' He was right – it did!

4 Speak

Think of a famous scientist from your country.

- When did he/she live? • Why is he/she famous?

Study tip

Writing in paragraphs

A paragraph contains one topic or idea. You start a new paragraph when you change the topic or idea. A composition usually has more than one paragraph.

How many paragraphs are there in the text about Copernicus in Exercise 3? Which paragraph is about:
- The book he wrote?
- What one person thought of his theory?
- His early life and education?

Project — Portfolio

A famous scientist

Write three paragraphs about a famous scientist.

Paragraph 1: his/her early life
- When and where was he/she born?
- Where did he/she live?
- Where and what did he/she study?

Paragraph 2: why he/she is famous
- What did he/she say or discover?
- Why was this important?

Paragraph 3: the end of his/her life
- When, where and how did he/she die?

Charles Darwin was an English scientist. He was born in 1809 in …

10 Revision

1 Look at the pictures and complete the text about Ollie's mum with *could* or *couldn't* and the verb.

① run + ✓

② jump + ✓

③ swim + ✓

④ hit + ✗

⑤ kick + ✗

⑥ skateboard + ✗

When I was a child in Australia I was very good at some sports but I was really bad at others. I was a good runner. For example, I ¹*could run* 100 metres in 12 seconds. I ²... two metres. I was a good swimmer too. I ³... a kilometre, no problem. But I wasn't so good at ball sports. I ⁴... a tennis ball, for example, and I ⁵... a football. Oh, and there's one more thing I couldn't do – I ⁶... !

2 <u>Underline</u> the mistake and write the correct verb form.

Amy: I <u>was seeing</u> Ella yesterday.	1 *saw*
Dan: Oh, what were she doing?	2 ...
Amy: She walked in the park.	3 ...
Dan: Did she sees you?	4 ...
Amy: No, she talked to a friend.	5 ...
Dan: Who did she talk to?	6 ...
Amy: A boy. I wasn't knowing him.	7 ...
Dan: Were he wearing a red baseball cap?	8 ...
Amy: Yes, he was. How were you knowing?	9 ...
Dan: I was meeting him last week. He's cool.	10 ...

3 Complete the text with verbs in the past simple or the past continuous.

Yesterday Emily ¹*was having* (have) breakfast when the phone ²*rang* (ring) It ³... (be) her friend Laura. 'What ⁴... (do) when I rang?' Laura ⁵... (ask). Emily ⁶... (say) she ⁷... (finish) her breakfast. They ⁸... (start) to talk. Two hours later Emily's dad ⁹... (come) into the kitchen. Emily and Laura ¹⁰... still (talk).

4 🎧 Sounds fun /ʊ/ and /uː/

Listen and repeat.

He looked at the book
Then took a big spoon
And drummed a new tune
In the light of the moon.

5 Look at the pictures and unscramble the prepositions.

George went for a walk in the park yesterday. First he walked ¹TASP *past* an old tree. Then he walked ²GLANO ... a river until he came to a gate. He opened the gate and walked ³HOGURTH ... a small field until he came to another gate. Then he went ⁴DUREN ... a bridge and then ⁵TION ... a different part of the park. After that he walked ⁶DURONA ... a small pond. Finally he walked ⁷UTO FO ... the park and went home.

6 Complete these sentences about an old man, Ted. Use forms of *used to*.

When he was a young man, Ted's hair ¹*used to be* (be) black. Now it's grey. He ²... (play) football but now he only watches it on TV. What else ³... he ... (do)? He ⁴... (dance) all evening and he ⁵... (not come) home until two o'clock. Now he usually goes to bed before ten. How ⁶... he ... (travel) when he was young? He ⁷... (cycle) or walk everywhere. He ⁸... (not drive) because he didn't have a car. Now he drives everywhere. But of course he says things ⁹... (be) much better when he was young.

7 Game

Complete the names of the musical instruments.

```
1 D R U M S
2   L   E
3   A
4   I   I
5 R   B
6   M   I
7 E   O
8   C R
9   O   N
```

8 🔊 Chat time

a) Talk to a friend. Follow the cues and write a conversation. Then act it out.

Student A	Student B
Ask how much English Student B could speak when he/she came to this school.	Say how much English you could speak.
Ask what sports Student B could/couldn't do.	Say what sports you could/couldn't do.
Ask which school Student B used to go to.	Say which school you used to go to.
Ask if Student B used to learn English at that school.	Say if you used to learn English at that school.

b) Listen to two girls talking. Compare your conversation with the girls' conversation.

What can you do?

I can:

- ask and talk about what you could/couldn't do as a child ☐
- ask and say what you were doing at certain times ☐
- ask and talk about your life now and in the past ☐
- ask and talk about famous people ☐

11 It isn't warm enough.

1 🎧 1/28 Listen and read

Rose, Jake and Jess are choosing clothes for a 1950s fancy dress party.

Jess: I want to wear my new mini skirt.
Jake: Mini skirts are too modern. They didn't wear mini skirts then.
Rose: Mum says she's got some 1950s clothes in her wardrobe.

A few minutes later

Jess: Hey, look. Can I try this pink anorak on?
Rose: Sure.
Jess: No, it's too big. I need a smaller size.
Rose: What about this spotted skirt?
Jess: It's OK but I hate tight belts.
Rose: What do you think of this dress?
Jess: It's nice but it's a bit flowery.

Jake and Mrs Spencer arrive

Rose: Are you going to wear that checked shirt? It's not very cool.
Jake: No. I'm going to wear a white T-shirt, jeans and a black leather jacket.
Rose: Very casual! It's so easy for boys! Mum, is this dress OK for the party?
Mum: Yes, but it's not warm enough. Perhaps you can wear a cardigan?
Rose: Oh Mum! You're so old-fashioned!

Now listen and repeat.

Everyday phrases
▯ Can I try this [pink anorak] on?
▯ What about [this spotted skirt]?
▯ What do you think of [this dress]?
▯ It's a bit [flowery].
▯ You're so [old-fashioned]!

2 🎧 New words: Clothes, patterns and styles

a) Listen and repeat.

Clothes
• coat • sweater • anorak • tracksuit • mini skirt
• cardigan • vest • shorts • sandals • belt

Patterns
• striped • checked • patterned • spotted
• flowery • plain

Styles
• baggy • loose • tight • short • long • smart
• casual

b) Use the words in a) to describe the clothes.

1 It's a checked coat.

3 Check

Correct the sentences.

1 ~~Rose~~ wants to try an anorak on. *Jess*
2 Rose hates tight belts.
3 Jess is wearing a flowery dress.
4 Jake is going to wear a checked shirt.

Look and learn

Too/enough
It's **too** big.
It's **not** warm **enough**.

Think about language
Before or after?
The word **too** comes *before/after* an adjective.
The word **enough** comes *before/after* an adjective.

---

4 Speak

Ask and answer questions about the clothes.
Use *too* or *not ... enough* and these words:

1 jeans/short 2 anorak/warm 3 coat/tight
4 belt/long 5 shorts/smart 6 trousers/baggy

A: *What do you think of these jeans?*
B: *They're too short.*

5 🎧 English in action: Shopping for clothes

a) Use these phrases to complete the dialogue.
Listen and check your answers.

• The changing rooms • Can I • Why don't
• What about • too small • size 12

A: ¹*What about* this blue sweater?
B: What size is it?
A: It's ²... .
B: ³... you try it on?
A: Excuse me. ⁴... try this blue sweater on, please?
C: Sure. ⁵... are over there.
B: Is it OK?
A: Sorry. It's ⁶... .

b) Practise the dialogue in groups of three.

You want to buy:
• a T-shirt • some shorts • a sweater • an anorak

6 Speak and write

a) Discuss in groups what clothes you wear for:

• a party • school • the gym • a friend's house

b) Make notes and write about what people said.

When Maria goes to a party she usually wears ...

A boy who becomes a spy.

12

STORMBREAKER

The plot

Stormbreaker is an action film about a 14-year-old schoolboy who becomes a teenage super spy. The boy, Alex Rider, lives with his uncle. His uncle dies very suddenly and Alex discovers that his uncle was really a spy who worked for the British secret service agency, MI6. The people at MI6 want Alex to work for them so they send him to a camp where he trains to be a spy. His task is to find Darius Sayle, a criminal who plans to kill the children of Britain. He is the inventor of a super computer which has a deadly virus. The computer is called 'Stormbreaker' and Darius Sayle plans to give Stormbreakers to every school in Britain. Alex tries to stop Sayle and save millions of lives.

The actors

A new young actor, Alex Pettyfer, plays Alex and Ewan McGregor plays his uncle. Mickey Rourke is excellent as Darius Sayle and Damian Lewis is very good as the enemy agent who kills Alex's uncle. This is an exciting and entertaining action film. It's definitely a film which is suitable for teenagers.

1 🎧 Read

Read about the film *Stormbreaker*.

2 Check

Match the two parts of the sentences.

1 d)

1	Alex Ryder	a)	is a computer.
2	Darius Sayle	b)	is a new, young actor.
3	Stormbreaker	c)	plays Darius Sayle.
4	Alex Pettyfer	d)	is a 14-year-old schoolboy.
5	Ewan McGregor	e)	is a criminal.
6	Mickey Rourke	f)	plays Alex's uncle.

3 🎧 New words: Film types

a) Listen and repeat. Then match.

1 science fiction

- cartoon/animated film • comedy • action film
- musical • western • horror film • fantasy film
- science fiction film • historical film

b) Think of examples of five different types of film. Compare your answers in pairs.

A: *Harry Potter is a fantasy film.*

B: *Star Wars is a science fiction film.*

4 Speak

Discuss in groups which types of film you like.

A: *Do you like horror films?*
B: *No, I don't. I like science fiction films and action films. How about you?*
A: *I like … .*

> **Look and learn**
>
> **Defining relative clauses with *who*, *which* and *where***
> Alex Ryder is a boy **who** lives with his uncle.
> It's an exciting film **which** is suitable for teenagers.
> He goes to a camp **where** he trains to be a spy.
>
> **Think about language**
> Which do we use for people: *who, which* or *where*?
> Which do we use for things: *who, which* or *where*?
> Which do we use for places: *who, which* or *where*?

5 Write

Complete the text about the film *Shrek the Third*. Use *who*, *which* or *where*.

The plot

Shrek the Third is an animated film ¹ *which* is about Shrek. He is a green ogre ² … is married to Princess Fiona. King Harold, Fiona's father is ill. He asks Shrek to be king. Shrek says no. Shrek and Donkey go to a school ³ … they find Arthur. He is a boy ⁴ … is the king's nephew.
Shrek says Arthur must be king but Prince Charming also wants to be king. Prince Charming and his men go to the castle ⁵ … Princess Fiona is living. Shrek fights Prince Charming and wins. Arthur becomes king.

The actors

Mike Myers ⁶ … is the voice of Shrek is good and Eddie Murphy ⁷ … is the voice of Donkey is very funny. It's a fantastic film ⁸ … is very popular.

6 Write

Use the film review in Exercise 1 and the text in Exercise 5 to help you.

My favourite film is X. It's an action film. It's about a man who … .

7 English in action: Buying cinema tickets

a) Listen and number the lines of the dialogue.

- [ ] How old are you?
- [ ] Which performance?
- [ ] The 4.30, please.
- [ ] I'm fourteen and my brother's twelve.
- [1] Can I have two tickets to see *Spider-Man 2*, please?
- [ ] That's OK. Right. That's £14, please.

b) Act out the dialogue using these films.

Casino Royale	2.30	4.30	7.00	9.15
Pirates of the Caribbean	3.00	5.15	8.00	9.30
Mr Bean's Holiday	2.15	5.00	7.00	9.15

All seats £7.00   Under 12 £5

8 Joke

I hate people who talk behind your back.

Yes, especially in the cinema!

There's something here.

1 New words: Shapes and textures

a) Listen and repeat.

1. round 2. hard 3. thin 4. straight 5. thick 6. bendy

7. square 8. dull 9. rough 10. shiny 11. smooth 12. soft

b) Which word is wrong a), b) or c)?

1 a)

1 A desk can be
a) bendy b) shiny c) hard

2 A table can be
a) square b) round c) soft

3 A sandwich can be
a) thick b) rough c) thin

4 A road can be
a) smooth b) dull c) straight

2 Read

School students find stolen sculpture in canal

Two fourteen-year-old teenagers were very happy when their fishing trip finished with more than a fish. Grant Sanderson and Robbie Clayton, from East London, decided to go fishing by the canal. 'There was nothing to watch on television,' explained Grant.

The boys fished for two hours but didn't catch anything. Suddenly Robbie saw something at the edge of the canal. 'It looked like a smooth black stone but when we picked it up, we realised it was more than that.' The 'stone' was quite long and shiny and it had a round hole through the top of it. 'It was on a square wooden base,' said Robbie. 'It looked quite valuable.'

'There was no one to ask,' said Grant, 'and we weren't anywhere near a police station so we took it home.' When they got home, Grant's mother phoned the police. It turned out that the 'stone' was a stolen sculpture by someone quite well-known. 'I expect the thieves who stole it didn't think it was worth anything so they threw

Now listen and repeat the first two paragraphs of the article.

3 Check

Number the events in the correct order.

a) Grant's mother phoned the police. ☐
b) Robbie pointed to a smooth black stone. ☐
c) Grant and Robbie decided to go fishing. *1*
d) They took the 'stone' home. ☐
e) They picked up the 'stone'. ☐
f) They fished for two hours. ☐

Look and learn

Someone/something/somewhere/; anyone/anything/anywhere; no one/nothing/nowhere

Positive
Someone threw it into the river.
He pointed to **something** shiny.
They threw it **somewhere**.

Negative
They couldn't see **anyone**.
They didn't catch **anything**.
They couldn't find a policeman **anywhere**.
There was **no one** to ask.
There was **nothing** on TV.
They were **nowhere** near a police station.

Questions
Did **anyone** see it?
Did they catch **anything**?
Did they take it **anywhere**?

Think about language
Something, anything or *nothing*?
We use ... for positive statements.
We use ... and ... for negative statements.
We use ... for questions.

4 Read and write

Read and complete the magazine article with a pronoun. Choose from:

• someone	• somewhere	• something	• anyone
• anywhere	• anything	• no one	• nowhere	• nothing

Believe it or not!

Eight years ago Jodie White had a dog and a cat. But she wanted ¹*something* a bit different. Her uncle gave her his tortoise. It was 30 years old. She called him Terence.

A month after she got him, Terence disappeared. 'Don't worry. He's ²... in the garden,' her dad said. But he wasn't. So they looked in their neighbour's garden but they couldn't find him ³.... When there was ⁴... else to look they agreed there was ⁵... more they could do. Jodie didn't say ⁶... but she never forgot Terence.

Last week ⁷... rang the Whites. Jodie answered the phone. 'It was our neighbour from eight years ago. He now lives in Swindon, fifteen kilometres away. He said there was a tortoise in his garden and didn't know ⁸... in the street with a lost tortoise. Could it be Terence?'

It was! But there's still a mystery. ⁹... can explain how Terence walked for fifteen kilometres across five busy roads, a railway line, a motorway, a canal and a river.

5 🎧 Listen

a) Listen to Rose and Jake playing a guessing game. First note Jake's questions and then note Rose's questions.

Jake	Rose
1 Is it someone famous?	1 Is it something to eat?
2 ...	2 ...
3 ...	3 ...
4 ...	4 ...

b) What were the answers?

6 Speak

Play the game in Exercise 5. Don't forget to give the first letter. You can ask ten *Yes/No* questions to guess the person or thing.

7 Did you know?

There are over 8,000 kilometres of canals in Britain. Many are over 200 years old. They are very narrow so canal boats are only two metres wide. But the boats can be seventeen metres long! These boats used to carry heavy materials like coal. Today people travel on them for a holiday.

Multicultural Britain

1 🎧 **37** **Read**

The people of Britain

Nowadays most big British cities have a mixture of races and cultures. This is what two teenagers from different ethnic minorities had to say.

'I'm British and I'm Pakistani too. My grandparents moved here about fifty years ago so my parents were born here and, of course, I was born here too. At home we speak Urdu because my mum and dad think it's important for us to keep our culture. We usually eat Pakistani food – things like chicken shashlik and vegetable curry. I usually wear European clothes but on special occasions I wear a traditional salwar kameez – it's a pair of trousers with a long top.

My dad is a computer engineer and my mum's a nurse. They say school is very important because they want me to go to university when I'm older.

Last year I visited Pakistan for the first time. I stayed with my cousins.'

Gita, 13

Gita, 13, lives with her parents and two brothers.

'I live two lives: one at home and the other at school. We live in a very British semi-detached house but inside it's like a home in Hong Kong! There are lots of Chinese pictures and furniture, my mum and grandmother normally cook Chinese food and we watch Chinese TV on satellite. We speak Cantonese with each other and, of course, we celebrate Chinese New Year.

At school I'm the only Chinese student but when I'm with my school friends I'm just one of them – we all laugh about the same things and we like the same music and clothes. My parents both work in our family's restaurant but they don't want me or my sisters to work there. They want us to get a good education so we can get well-paid jobs.

I suppose I live in two cultures at the same time but I think it's important to take the good things from every community. For example, I like the Chinese tradition of looking after older people and I like the freedom British teenagers have.'

Shing Wei, 14

Shing Wei, 14, lives with his grandmother, mother, father and two sisters.

FACT FILE

- The population of Britain is about 60.6 million.
- One out of eight British people is from a minority ethnic group, that is 4.5 million people.
- The biggest ethnic groups are from India, Pakistan, Bangladesh, the West Indies, Africa and China. Most of them live in big cities like London, Birmingham and Leicester.
- Many people from different countries in the European Union now live and work in Britain.

New words

- multicultural • nowadays • mixture • races • cultures
- ethnic • minority • curry • occasions • satellite
- New Year • laugh • education • well-paid • community
- tradition • freedom • population • European Union

2 Check

Right (✓), wrong (✗) or don't know (DK)?

1 Gita's from Pakistan. ✗
2 She never wears Pakistani clothes.
3 She wants to go to university.
4 Six people live in Shing Wei's house.
5 Shing Wei can speak Cantonese.
6 He thinks British teenagers get a lot of freedom.

3 🎧 Listen

Choose the right answer.

1 Gita talks about her a) brothers b) parents c) grandparents
2 They live a) in Pakistan b) with Gita's parents
  c) in their own house
3 Gita wants to be a) a nurse b) a teacher c) an engineer
4 Shing Wei lives in a) London b) Liverpool c) Manchester
5 His sisters are a) 11 and 12 b) 12 and 13 c) 15 and 16
6 At university he wants to study a) Maths b) Medicine
  c) Computer engineering

4 Speak

What are the ethnic communities in your country?

- Where do they live?
- Are their food, language, clothes and lifestyles different from yours?

Project | Portfolio

The people of my country

Writing tip

Linkers *so/because*
We use linkers to join sentences. When one sentence is the result or cause of the other, you link the sentences with *so* or *because*.

We speak Urdu *because* it's important to keep our culture.

It's important to keep our culture *so* we speak Urdu.

Find one more example with *because* and two with *so* in Exercise 1.

Write a website about one of the ethnic communities in your country. Use these topics:

- language • clothes • food
- lifestyle

> The people of my country
> There are many people from different ethnic communities in my country. One of these groups of people is Chinese.

15 Revision

1 Complete the crossword with the patterns.

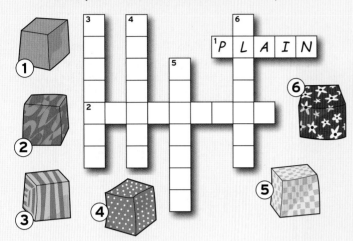

¹P L A I N

2 Sounds fun /aɪ/

Listen, then listen and repeat.

The red and white striped top
Is very bright,
But it's my size and I like it!

3 The Lee family went to a fast food place. Complete what they said with *too* and *n't (not) enough*.

Jenny: My chips were ¹*too cold* (cold).
Nicky: My fish was ²... (hot). In fact it was cold.
Mr Lee: My burger was quite small. It definitely was ³... (big) for me!
Jenny: I agree. My burger was ⁴... (small).
Mrs Lee: The waiters were ⁵... (slow).
Mr Lee: Yes, our food took ⁶... (long) to come.
Mrs Lee: And the place was ⁷... (noisy).
Nicky: And our table was quite small. It definitely was ⁸... (big) for the four of us.
Mr Lee: And it was ⁹... (expensive). We'll never come here again.

4 Find the eight types of film in the wordsnake.

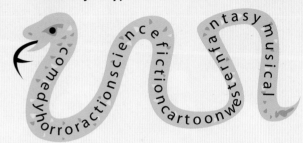

1 comedy

5 Make sentences about a boy's holiday photos with *who*, *which* or *where*.

1 The plane *which* we flew on was very big.
2 The campsite ... we stayed was OK.
3 This is the tent ... we slept in.
4 The boys ... we met were nice.
5 The café ... we ate in was clean.
6 The waiter ... served us was friendly.
7 The beach ... we played volleyball was beautiful.

6 Complete the conversation with these words.

- old • That's • performance • tickets
- seven o'clock • fourteen • see

A: Can we have four ¹*tickets* to ²... *Stormbreaker*, please?
B: How ³... are you?
A: We're all ⁴... .
B: Which ⁵...?
A: The ⁶..., please.
B: All right. ⁷... £24, please.

7 Underline the correct answer.

Sophie and Amy were on a cycling holiday, ¹*somewhere/ anywhere* in Ireland. They stopped in a small village. It was hot and they were thirsty and they had ²*no one/nothing* to drink. They looked for a café but there wasn't one ³*anyone/ anywhere*. They thought about asking ⁴*someone/anyone* but there was ⁵*no one/nothing* to ask. But then they saw a village shop. Surely they could buy ⁶*something/somewhere* to drink in there. But there wasn't ⁷*no one/anyone* in the shop. There was just a sign on the door. It said, 'If ⁸*no one/nowhere* is here, we're closed.'

8 Match the opposite adjectives.

1 d)

① **square**
② **rough**
③ **straight**
④ **shiny**
⑤ **thick**
⑥ **hard**

ⓐ **dull**
ⓑ **soft** ⓒ **bendy**
ⓓ **round**
ⓔ **smooth**
ⓕ **thin**

9 🎧 Chat time

a) You are shopping. In pairs, follow the cues and write a conversation. Then act it out.

A: *Excuse me. Can I try these jeans on, please?*
B: *Yes, the changing rooms …*

Student A	Student B
You find some jeans you like. Ask the assistant if you can try them on.	Say yes. Say where the changing rooms are.
Thank the assistant.	Ask if the jeans are OK.
Say what's wrong with them. Ask if he/she has got a bigger/smaller size.	Apologise. Say you've only got that size.
Thank the assistant and leave.	

b) Listen to Shilpa talking to an assistant and compare your conversation.

10 Puzzle: Who's Who?

Who's wearing what? Read the descriptions and write the name of the person.

Will   Chloe   Emily   Richard   Laura   Betsy

1 A flowery skirt and a checked vest. *Chloe*
2 A patterned coat with a belt.
3 A striped sweater and a mini skirt.
4 Shorts and sandals.
5 A spotted cardigan under an anorak.
6 A plain tracksuit.

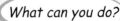

What can you do?

I can:

• talk about clothes you like and don't like ☐
• talk about films ☐
• buy cinema tickets ☐
• ask questions to play a guessing game ☐

1  Listen and read

The friends are watching their school team play against another school team.

Ranu: Hi guys! Do you want a hot dog?
Rose: No thanks. We've already had one.
Jake: So, have we scored yet?
Ranu: No, we're useless today!

Later

Ranu: Oh no! They've just scored.
Jake: They're going to beat us. I know it.
Rose: Don't be silly! There are still fifteen minutes to go.
Jake: Come on, Joe. Put the ball in the net! Yes!
Rose: That's good. The score's one all.
Ranu: Yes. But we don't want to draw, we want to win!
Jake: There's still a chance!
Ranu: Dream on!
Jake: Yes, yes, yes!! That's the best goal I've ever seen!
Rose: You always say that!
Ranu: Don't celebrate too soon. The match hasn't finished yet.

Now listen and repeat.

Everyday phrases

- Hi guys!
- We're useless!
- Come on [Joe]!
- Put the ball in the net!
- That's good.
- There's still a chance.
- Dream on!
- You always say that!

2 Check

Right (✓), wrong (✗) or don't know (DK)?

1 The friends are watching a football match. ✓
2 They all go to the same school. ✗
3 Rose and Jake want another hot dog. ✗
4 A boy called Joe gets a goal. ✓
5 The friends' school win the match. ✗

3 New words: Words to do with sports

a) Listen and repeat.

- match • tournament • team • whistle (n)
- score (n) • pass (v) • tackle (v) • play (v)
- draw (n) • score (v) • beat (v) • win (v)
- lose (v) • draw (v) • stop

b) How many of the words can you find in the dialogue?

Look and learn

Present perfect simple with *just*, *already* and *yet*

Positive   **Negative**
Beckton have **just** scored.   The match hasn't finished **yet**.
We've **already** had one.

Question
Have we scored **yet**? Yes, we have./No, we haven't.

Think about language
Just, already or *yet*?
Which word is positioned at the end of a sentence?

4 Write

Make a chart with the infinitives of the past participles in the box.

| • known • won • beaten • made • lost • scored • bought |
| • found • played • done • seen • come • had • became |

Infinitive	Past participle
know	*known*

5 Speak

Work in pairs. In turns say what's just happened in one picture. Your partner says which picture it is.

A: *She's just won £500.*
B: *Picture 4.*
  He's ...

The Stars/lose/match

He/score/goal

She/win/£500

They/have/dinner

He/buy/computer game

6 Act

a) It's 6 o'clock on Saturday evening. Rose and Jess are talking on the phone. Act the dialogue.

Rose: *Have you done your homework yet?*
Jess: *Yes, I have. Have you had your supper yet?*
Rose: *...*

Jess

done/homework ✓
see/the website for the concert ✓
buy/tickets ✗

Rose

have/supper ✗
wash/hair ✓
found/mobile ✓

b) Say what the girls have or haven't done using *yet* or *already*.

Jess has already done her homework and she ... but she ... .

7 Listen

Ollie is going out but his mum wants to know what he's already done or hasn't done yet. Listen and write ✓✓ for *done*, ✓ for *just done* or ✗ for *not done yet*. Then tell the class.

1 *He's just tidied his room.*

1 tidy/his room ✓
2 finish/his homework
3 help/Jess
4 phone/his grandmother
5 buy/a birthday card

17 I've never done that.

1 🎧 New words: Travel

a) Listen and repeat.

- double-decker bus • scooter
- plane • mountain bike • taxi
- motorbike • (long distance) coach
- caravan • lorry • helicopter
- high-speed train • ferry

b) Match. Which words aren't in the pictures?

1 mountain bike

c) Sort the different forms of transport in a) into three groups.

Land	Air	Sea
train		

2 🎧 Read and listen

a) Read Jess and Rose's answers to questions 1 and 2 in the questionnaire and tick the correct box.

Jess: Hey, Rose. Let's do this travel questionnaire. Question 1, 'Have you ever been on a double-decker bus?'

Rose: Yes, I have. In London.

Jess: Me too. Next question, 'Have you ever ridden a scooter?'

Rose: No, I've never done that. I've never ridden a scooter or a motorbike.

Jess: I've ridden a friend's scooter in a car park. It was great.

TRAVEL QUESTIONNAIRE

Tick the box if you've ever done these things.

Have you ever:

		Rose	Jess
1	been on a double-decker bus?	☐	☐
2	ridden a scooter?	☐	☐
3	travelled all night on a plane?	☐	☐
4	ridden a mountain bike?	☐	☐
5	gone anywhere by taxi?	☐	☐
6	ridden on the back of a motorbike?	☐	☐
7	travelled a long distance by coach?	☐	☐
8	had a caravan holiday?	☐	☐
9	flown in a helicopter?	☐	☐

b) Now listen to their answers to questions 3-9 and fill in the rest of the questionnaire.

Look and learn

Present perfect simple with *ever* and *never*

Have you **ever** ridden a scooter?
Yes, I **have**. I rode a scooter last month.
No, I **haven't**. I've **never** ridden a scooter.

Have you **ever** been on a high-speed train?
Yes, I **have**. I went on one last year.
No, I **haven't**. I've never been on one.

Think about language
We use *ever/never* for questions.
We use *ever/never* for the negative.

3 Write

Find the past participles of these verbs in the questionnaire and complete the chart.

Infinitive	Past participle
1 be	*been*
2 ride	...
3 travel	...
4 go	...
5 have	...
6 fly	...

4 Speak

a) Look at Jake and Ollie's answers to some of the questionnaire. In pairs, ask and answer questions.

A: *Have Jake and Ollie ever been on a double-decker bus?*
B: *Yes, they have.*
A: *Has Jake ever ridden a scooter?*
B: *No, he hasn't.*

	Jake	Ollie
1 be/on a double-decker bus?	✓	✓
2 ride/a scooter?	✗	✓
3 go/anywhere/by taxi	✓	✗
4 travel/by coach?	✓	✓
5 have/a caravan holiday?	✗	✓
6 fly/in a helicopter?	✗	✗

b) Ask a friend the same questions.

c) Tell the class about your friend.

Ania has travelled on a long distance coach but she's never flown in a helicopter.

5 Read and write

a) Read and complete this postcard with the correct form of the verb.

I ¹ *'m* at Alton Towers. I ² ... (never/be) here before but I ³ ... (hear) a lot about it. ⁴ ... (you/ever/be?) We ⁵ ... (come) here by coach this morning – It ⁶ ... (be) a long trip! So far I ⁷ ... (go) on three big rides. They ⁸ ... (be) SCARY! Oh, and I ⁹ ... (have) a pizza and two hamburgers for lunch! See you! Tom

b) Write a postcard to a friend. Imagine that you are visiting somewhere for the first time.

Portfolio

6 Listen

Listen and complete the information.

Transport from Heathrow Airport to Central London		
	Time	**Cost**
Taxi	1 *50 minutes*	2 *£45*
Train	3 ...	4 ...
Bus	5 ...	6 ...
Underground	7 ...	8 ...

7 English in action: Buying a ticket

a) Listen then practise the conversation.

A: *Can I have a ticket to Central London, please?*
B: *Single or return?*
A: *Single, please.*
B: *That's £15.*
A: *When does the next train leave?*
B: *It leaves at 14.25.*
A: *Thank you.*

b) Act out a similar conversation using information in the table in Exercise 6.

8 Song: *Have you Ever?* by S Club 7

Go to page 93 and listen and join in the song.

1 🎧 (2/07) Listen and read

Ollie has arranged to meet Jake and Rose at the school book club.

Ollie: Hi. Sorry I'm late.

Jake: That's OK. Come and sit down.

Ollie: How long have you been here?

Jake: Since half past three. I've already chosen my book.

Ollie: What are you going to read?

Jake: This book of ghost stories. It's been top of the book club list for three weeks.

Ollie: I haven't read it yet. Can I have it after you?

Jake: Sure.

Ollie: I want to read the seventh Harry Potter. Is it here?

Rose: No, it isn't. I haven't seen it in the library for ages. I think Ranu borrowed it. Why don't you read this science fiction story? It's brilliant.

Ollie: Cool. Thanks.

Jake: OK. Let's go now and get something to eat. I'm starving.

Ollie: Don't exaggerate! You had lunch two hours ago!

Now listen and repeat.

Everyday phrases

- Sorry I'm late.
- That's OK.
- Come and sit down.
- [I haven't seen it] for ages.
- It's brilliant.
- Don't exaggerate!

2 Check

Correct the sentences.

1 Ollie ~~isn't~~ late. *is*
2 Jake came at 4.00.
3 Rose's going to read some ghost stories.
4 Ollie borrowed a Harry Potter book.
5 Rose tells Ollie to read a detective story.

Look and learn

Present perfect simple with *for* and *since*

Question
How long have you been here?

Positive
I've been here **since** 3.30/**for** half an hour.

Negative
I haven't seen it **since** last month/**for** ages.

Think about language
For or *since*?
• two weeks • last summer • two years
• 10 o'clock • Monday night

---

3 Write

Work in pairs. Complete the second sentence with the present perfect and *for* or *since*.

1 **A:** Ollie and Jess came to England in June.
   B: They *'ve been* (be) here *for* six months.
2 **B:** Jess was twelve when she came.
   A: She … (be) here …. she was twelve.
3 **B:** Jake bought his mobile two months ago.
   A: He … (have) it … two months.
4 **A:** They became friends a few months ago.
   B: They … (be) friends … a few months.

4 Speak

Work in pairs. Ask questions with *How long …?* Answer with *for* or *since*.

1 **A:** *How long have you been at this school?*
   B: *I've been here for two years.*

1 How long/you/be/at this school?
2 How long/you/know/your friend X?
3 How long/you/live/in this town?
4 How long/your parents/live/here?

5 New words: Types of book

Listen and repeat.

• detective story • fantasy book • ghost story
• short story • adventure story • romantic novel
• science fiction book • biography • historical novel
• fairy tale

6 Read

Listen and read the text about *The Horse Whisperer*.

My favourite book

My favourite book is *The Horse Whisperer* by Nicholas Evans. It's a romantic novel about a 13-year-old girl, Grace, and her horse, Pilgrim. Both horse and rider are badly hurt when a truck hits them. Grace loses a leg and the horse nearly dies. The girl's mother takes them to the mountains in the west of the USA. There she finds a man, a horse whisperer called Tom Booker. After they have been with him for some time, both girl and horse slowly get better. I haven't read such a fantastic book for a long time. Since I read it, I have seen the film with Robert Redford and Scarlett Johansson. I think the book's better than the film!
Jenny Franklin

7 Check

Complete the information.

Title: *The Horse Whisperer*	Author:
Type of book:	Main characters:
Main story:	Why I like it:

8 Speak

Talk about the books you like.

I like science fiction. I think I've read more than twenty science fiction novels. I don't like adventure stories or romantic novels.

9 Write

Write about one of your favourite books. Use Exercise 6 to help you.

Portfolio

Across Australia by train

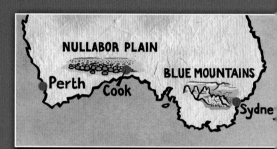

1 🎧 ²⁄₁₀ **Read**

Australia's a huge country. You can see a lot of it from a train called the Indian Pacific. It travels 4,352 km from Sydney on the east coast to Perth on the west coast. It takes three days and nights. Charlie (14) went on this train with his parents and he wrote a diary.

Saturday 14th January
We've left Sydney and we're crossing the Blue Mountains. We can see mountains, rivers, forests and lakes. It's beautiful. But we haven't seen any kangaroos yet.

Sunday morning
We've just left the Blue Mountains and it's much flatter. It's farming country with thousands of sheep and cows, and kangaroos! Some really big red ones tried to race us. They were fast but we were faster.

Monday morning
We've been on the train for 34 hours. We're crossing the Nullabor Plain. It's a huge, empty red desert. Near the railway line there's a very bumpy, narrow track and I've just seen a motorcyclist on it. He must be crazy!

Monday afternoon
We've just stopped in a very small town called Cook. Its population is only 40 and it has no roads, only the railway. I'm glad I'm not a teenager living in Cook. Boring or what!

Monday evening
I've seen some wild camels. Australians used to use them for transport across the desert. Now they use the train instead. I've just had my first crocodile steak. Mum and Dad didn't dare eat it!

Tuesday 9.10
We've arrived in Perth. It looks very like Sydney! One piece of advice. If you want to travel on the Indian Pacific, don't miss your train. The next one won't leave for another three days.

Facts about Australia

Population:	20.6 million
Size:	The world's sixth biggest country.
Geography:	The world's lowest, driest, flattest continent.
People:	People have lived in Australia for 50,000 years. Europeans have lived there since 1770. 23% of Australians were born overseas. Most have come from Italy, Greece, Vietnam and China. Only 2.2% of Australians are aborigines.

New words

• lowest • flattest • continent • overseas • aborigines
• farming • race (v) • desert • bumpy • narrow • track
• motorcyclist • crazy • camel • transport • advice • miss

Study tip

Guessing the meaning of words
When you read a text, try to guess the meaning of new words. First decide if the word is a noun, verb, adjective or adverb. Then look at the other words in the sentence and the sentences before and after. If you can't guess, use a dictionary or ask your teacher.

Look at the new words in the sentences below from the text. Can you guess what they mean?
Near the railway line there's a very <u>bumpy, narrow track</u> and I've just seen a <u>motorcyclist</u> on it. He must be <u>crazy</u>!

2 Check

Complete the chart. Tick (✓) the correct column.

When did it happen?	Saturday	Sunday	Monday	Tuesday
1 Charlie saw some camels.			✓	
2 They arrived in Perth.				
3 Charlie ate a crocodile steak.				
4 He saw his first kangaroo.				
5 He left Sydney.				
6 He saw a crazy motorcyclist.				

3 🎧 Listen

Listen to Charlie talking to a friend back in England about the next part of their journey round Australia. Choose the correct answer.

1 How long are they going to stay in Perth?
   a) one day b) two days
   c) three days
2 How are they going to travel to Ayers Rock?
   a) by bus b) by train c) by plane
3 How high is Ayers Rock?
   a) 200 metres b) 300 metres c) 400 metres
4 How far round is it?
   a) eight kilometres b) nine kilometres c) ten kilometres
5 What time are they going to start climbing?
   a) at 5 o'clock b) at 6 o'clock c) at 9 o'clock

4 Speak

Tell the class about a long journey you went on. Use the questions to help you.

• Where did you go?
• How long did you stay?
• How did you travel?
• Who did you go with?

Project Portfolio

An interesting trip

Imagine you have just come back from a long trip. Draw a map and mark your route. Write about:

• how you travelled
• some of the things that happened

An interesting trip
Last summer we went on the Eurostar train through the Channel Tunnel to Paris. We stayed in Paris for two days and went to the top of the Eiffel Tower. The view was fantastic! Then we took the train all the way through France to Italy ...

20 Revision

1 Complete the words.

1. W I N
2. P _ _ S
3. P _ _ Y
4. B _ _ T
5. L _ _ E
6. D _ _ W
7. M _ _ _ H
8. S _ _ _ E
9. T _ _ _ _ E
10. T _ _ _ N _ _ _ T

Clues

1. We want to *win* .
2. ... the ball to me.
3. We didn't ... well.
4. We ... them 3-2.
5. Oh no! We're going to ...
6. It was a ... - 3-3.
7. It was a good ...
8. I didn't ... a goal.
9. If he's got the ball, ... him!
10. We're in the final of the ...

2 Complete the missing forms of the verbs.

	Verb	Past	Past Participle
1	be	was/were	*been*
2	beat	...	beaten
3	become	...	become
4	...	bought	bought
5	come	...	come
6	...	did	done
7	drive	drove	...
8	fly	flew	...
9	...	found	found
10	go	...	gone
11	have	...	had
12	know	knew	...
13	...	lost	lost
14	...	made	made
15	ride	rode	...
16	see	...	seen
17	...	travelled	travelled
18	...	won	won

3 Complete the conversation with the present perfect simple.

Ollie: Hello Mrs Spencer. This is Ollie. Can I speak to Jake please?

Mrs S: I'm sorry, Ollie. ¹*He's just gone out.* (He/just/go out)

Ollie: Oh, no. ²... (Rose/leave/yet)?

Mrs S: No, she's doing her homework and ³... (she/not/finish/yet). Oh, wait a minute. She says ⁴... (she/just/finish) it. Here she is.

Rose: Hi, Ollie. Did Mum tell you? ⁵... (Jake/already/leave) and ⁶... (I/just/do) my homework. ⁷... (I/already/arrange) to meet Jess at half past ten. Do you want to come too?

Ollie: No, it's OK thanks. ⁸... (I/just/have) a text message from another friend. I'm meeting him at 11.

Rose: That's OK then. See you.

4 Write the complete conversation. Use the present perfect simple.

Adam: ¹*Have you ever been* (you/ever/be) to a foreign country?

Toby: Yes, I ²... . I ³... (be) to France and Spain.

Adam: ⁴... (you/ever/fly)?

Toby: Yes, I ⁵... (fly) three times. How about you?

Adam: No, I ⁶... (never/fly). But my older sister ⁷... (fly) lots of times. She ⁸... (be) to ten different countries. But I ⁹... (travel) on a high-speed train. It was great!

5 Odd word out. <u>Underline</u> the word which does not go with the other two.

1 airport/<u>caravan</u>/plane
2 train/station/flight
3 ride/scooter/station
4 get off/drive/car
5 get on/take off/bus
6 gate/airport/boat
7 taxi/road/flight
8 station/platform/fly
9 helicopter/bus/plane
10 leave/scooter/arrive

6  Sounds fun /eɪ/

Listen, then listen and repeat.

Kate is waiting at gate number eight
To get on the plane to Spain.

7 a) Put these phrases in the right column.

• Monday morning • three days • a week • last September • 2005 • she was born • a long time • a month

Since	For
Monday morning	*three days*

b) Complete the sentences with the present perfect simple and *for* or *since*.

1 I (know) *have known* Nick *for* three years.
2 My grandmother (have) ... a mobile ... last June.
3 Emma (not/speak) ... to me ... a week.
4 Two of my friends (be) ... away from school ... Tuesday.
5 I (live) ... in this town ... a year.

8 These are the first lines of nine different types of book. What are they? Choose from:

• a detective story • a fairy tale • a romantic novel • a science fiction book • a ghost story • an adventure story • a biography • a historical novel • a fantasy book

1 Peter picked up his magic hat and flew round the room.
   A fantasy book
2 Charlie Chaplin was born on 16th April 1889.
3 The spacecraft opened and four green men got out.
4 'Where were you yesterday?' the detective asked.
5 'I love you,' Charles said to her.
6 The twelve princesses danced all night.
7 It was two o'clock when she heard the strange noise.
8 William knew he must climb the high mountain, but how?
9 On 20th July 1614, Josiah Jackman went to America.

9  Chat time

a) Write the conversation at a train station. Then act it out.

A: *Can I have a ticket to London, please?*
B: *Single or return?*

Student A	Student B

Ask Student B for a ticket to London.

> Ask if Student A wants a single or return ticket.

Say you would like a single ticket.

> Say it costs £20.

Ask what time the next train leaves.

> Say that it leaves at 16.30.

Ask what platform it leaves from.

> Say it leaves from platform 2.

Thank Student B.

b) Now listen to Mrs Martinez buying a ticket and compare your conversation.

What can you do?

I can:
- talk about what has just happened ☐
- ask and talk about past experiences ☐
- ask and talk about the past up to now ☐
- talk about the books I like ☐

21 What will they be like?

Listen and read about how computers will change our lives in the 21st century.

Small is beautiful

In the 21st century, how will computers change our lives?

Katherine Ross reports

Technology develops all the time. Scientists predict that in the next twenty years, people won't have just one PC at home, they will have several computers. What will they be like? Will they all be laptops? No, they won't. Some of them will be tiny and people will wear them on their clothes and under their skin.

Computers will also do different things. They will help you to shop faster on the Internet. At the moment, when you want to buy some new trainers on the Internet, you have to search the Web. In the future, you will show your laptop a picture of the trainers that you want and the computer will find the right websites immediately.

What's more, you won't need a mouse, a keyboard or a pen to communicate with your PC. You will talk to it. Also, it will understand your mood. When you are unhappy, it will play cheerful music.

Scientists predict too that computers will soon be able to help disabled people. With a microchip in their brain they will be able to control objects like the kitchen cooker or the TV by thinking alone. So when a disabled person thinks 'I want to watch TV', the brain chip will send a signal to turn the TV on.

2 New words: Technology

Listen and repeat. Then match five of the words.

1 keyboard

- laptop   • PC (personal computer)   • mouse
- screen   • monitor   • keyboard   • modem
- disc   • memory   • software   • website
- send/receive an email   • surf the Internet
- send/receive a text message   • search the Web
- connect to the Internet   • download music
- download software   • microchip

Look and learn

Future simple for prediction
will ('ll) and will not (won't)

Positive
People **will** have several computers.

Negative
People **won't** have just one computer.

Question
What **will** they be like?

Yes/No questions
Will they all be laptops?
Yes, they **will**./No, they **won't**.

Think about language
The short form of *will* is ...
The short form of *will not* is ...

3 Check

Answer the questions about the text in Exercise 1.

1 Will the average family have one computer?
2 Where will people wear computers?
3 How will computers help you to shop?
4 How will computers help you when you are sad?
5 How will disabled people be able to control their TV?

4 Read and speak

a) Read the predictions and note your opinion in the boxes: I agree (✓), I don't agree (✗) or I'm not sure (?).

What do you think will happen in the next twenty years?

Education
- Computers will replace teachers. ☒
- All students will have a laptop at school. ☑

Communication
- People won't send letters, they'll only send emails. ☑
- Phone boxes and post boxes will disappear completely. ☑

Space
- People will live on the moon. ☒
- The USA will send an astronaut to Mars. ☑

Transport
- Cars won't use petrol. They'll use electricity. ☑
- Planes will fly from London to Sydney in three hours. ☑

Health and beauty
- Many people will live until the age of 150. ☒
- Adults will go to a shop to choose a new face. ☒

b) In pairs, ask and answer about the predictions.

1 **A:** *Will computers replace teachers?*
   B: *Yes, they will./No, they won't./I'm not sure.*

c) Tell the class about your partner's answers.

In Marco's opinion, computers will replace teachers but people won't live on the moon.

5 Write

You are making a personal robot. Give it a name and say what five things it will do for you and some things it won't do.

My robot is called RoboFix. It will ... , but it won't ... .

22 I'll give you a hand.

1 🎧 2/16 Listen and read

Jake: Hi Ollie. I'm going to paint the walls in my room. Do you like this colour?

Ollie: Yes, it's good. I'll give you a hand if you like. Give me a paintbrush.

Mum: Jake?

Jake: Yes, Mum.

Mum: Are you all right? How's it going?

Jake: Fine.

Mum: Don't forget to take away the rug and the cushions before you start.

Jake: No, I won't. Don't worry.

Mum: And remember to put the paint pot in a safe place!

Jake: Yes, I will. I think I need to move the chest of drawers.

Ollie: Good idea. I'll help you. I'll take one end and you take the other.

Jake: There's someone at the door. I bet it's Ranu. I'll go and see. I won't be long. He's having a barbecue on Saturday and I've said I'll help him.

Ollie: Mind that paint pot!

Jake: Oh no! Mum will be really angry!

Now listen and repeat.

Everyday phrases

- I'll give you a hand.
- How's it going?
- Fine.
- Don't worry.
- Good idea.
- There's someone at the door.
- I bet [it's Ranu].
- Mind [that paint pot]!

2 Check

Complete the chart.

Who ...	Jake	Ollie	Mum
1 wants to paint his room?	✓		
2 offers to help him?			
3 wants to know how it's going?			
4 is worried about the rug and cushions?			
5 tells Jake to mind the paint pot?			

3 Memory check: Furniture

Find the eleven furniture words in the wordsquare. Then listen and check.

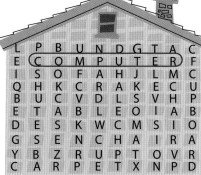

L P B U N D G T A C
E C O M P U T E R F
I S O F A H J L M C
Q H K C R A K E C U
B U C V D L S V H P
E T A B L E O I A B
D E S K W C M S I O
G S E N C H A I R A
Y B Z R U P T O V R
C A R P E T X N P D

4 New words: Furniture and furnishings

a) Listen and repeat.

- chest of drawers • wardrobe • lamp • curtains • rug
- cushion • mirror • waste bin • tablecloth • radiator
- blind(s)

b) Look at the photograph. Which things can you see?

I can see a chest of drawers, ...

Look and learn

Will/won't for offers, promises and decisions
I/We'**ll** help you.   I/We **won't** be long.

Remember to put the paint pot away.   Yes, I/we **will**.
Don't forget to take away the rug.   No, I/We **won't**.

---

5 Speak

You and your friends are planning a barbecue. Look at the list of things to do and offer to do things.

A: *I'll buy the food.*
B: *OK. I'll give you a hand.*

Things to do for the barbecue
- *buy food and drink*
- *set the table*
- *organise the music*
- *light the barbecue*
- *make the tomato sauce*
- *move garden furniture*
- *make the salad*
- *put up lights*
- *buy the charcoal*

6 English in action: Offering and reminding

a) Listen to the conversation.

A: *I'll invite our friends.*
B: *OK, I'll buy the food.*
A: *Magda, remember to buy the drink.*
C: *Yes, I will.*
A: *Georgio, don't forget to move the furniture.*
D: *No, I won't.*

b) Now plan your own barbecue or party. Make a list of things to do and discuss who will do what.

7 Listen

Listen to the telephone conversation. Complete the information.

Jess invites Rose and Jake to come to a ¹*barbecue*. It's on ²... at about ³... o'clock. Jess and Ollie have already got the ⁴... but they want Rose and Jake to bring some ⁵... and also a ⁶... .

8 Write

a) Rearrange the words of this email.

☰▾   Subject: Hi

1 Adam Hi!
2 on Saturday. a barbecue We're having
3 to come? Would like you
4 at 7.00. starts It
5 the sausages. buy We'll
6 some drinks? you bring Can
7 forget reply. to Don't
8 Lisa. Bye,

---

b) Write an invitation to a barbecue or party you're giving at your home.

Portfolio

9 Song: *Leaving on a Jet Plane* by John Denver

Go to page 93 and listen and join in the song.

23   I'd rather be a sports reporter.

1   Listen and read

Ollie: Wow! It's an amazing stadium!

Jake: I'd love a job here.

Rose: That's no surprise. You're football crazy.

Jess: Look. Here's a job for you, Jake. Programme seller!

Rose: Would you like to be a programme seller?

Jake: No, I wouldn't, thanks! What a boring job!

Jess: I'm not sure. They meet a lot of famous footballers!

Ollie: Typical! Which would you prefer to be, Jake? A footballer or a football manager?

Jake: Neither. I'd rather be a sports reporter. They travel a lot. I think it sounds interesting.

Jess: I'd like to be a politician.

Ollie: No wonder! You're so bossy.

Now listen and repeat.

Everyday phrases

- That's no surprise.
- You're [football] crazy.
- I'm not sure.
- I think it sounds [interesting].
- No wonder!
- You're so [bossy].

2 Check

Correct the sentences.

1 ~~Rose~~ is football crazy. *Jake*
2 There's a job for a hot dog seller.
3 Jake thinks it's a great job.
4 Jess thinks he'd probably meet a lot of famous pop stars.
5 Jake wants to be a footballer.
6 Jess would like to be a football manager.

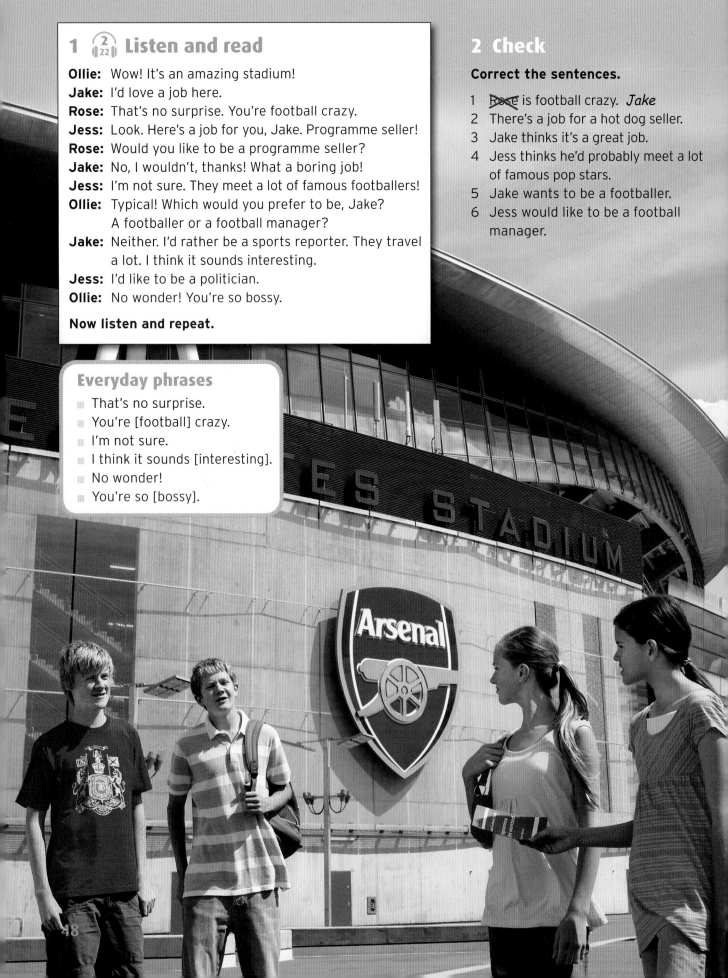

3 New words: Jobs

a) Listen and repeat.

- football manager • journalist • doctor
- TV reporter • TV newsreader
- politician • vet • model • plumber
- ski instructor • carpenter • hairdresser
- electrician • detective • police officer
- firefighter • pilot • footballer
- racing-car driver • web designer
- computer engineer • sports reporter

b) Match these things with eight of the jobs in a).

1	a newspaper	5	animals
2	hair	6	wood
3	a fire	7	a plane
4	mountains	8	clothes

1 a journalist

Look and learn

Modal: *would/wouldn't*

Positive
I**'d (would)** like to be a sports reporter.

Negative
I **wouldn't (would not)** like to be a politician.

Question
What **would** you like to be?

***Yes/No* questions**
Would you like to be a hairdresser?
Yes, I **would.**/No, I **wouldn't.**

Think about language
The short form of *would* is ...
The short form of *would not* is ...

---

4 Speak

Talk about your ambitions.

A: *What would you like to be?*
B: *I'd like to be a web designer because I enjoy working with computers.*

Look and learn

***Would rather/would prefer to* (preference)**
Which **would** you **rather** be/**would** you **prefer to** be, a footballer or a football manager?
I**'d rather** be a footballer. /I**'d prefer to** be a footballer.

---

5 Speak

Ask and answer about the jobs in Exercise 3.

A: *Which would you rather be, a vet or a doctor?*
B: *I'd rather be a vet./I'd prefer to be a vet.*

6 Listen

Listen to a quiz game called *Guess my job*. Can you guess the person's job before the member of the team?

7 Read

Read the article and complete the sentences.

1 Hannah wants to be a ... because ... .
2 Jason wants to be a ... or a ... because ... .

My Dream Job

I'd like to be a journalist. I'm quite good at English and I like talking to people and asking questions. The best thing about being a journalist is that every story is different so it would be very interesting. I wouldn't like to work for a London newspaper. London's so big! I'd prefer to stay here in Newcastle.

Hannah, 13, Newcastle

I'd like to be a police officer or a firefighter because I like helping people. I wouldn't like to work in an office, I'd prefer to be outside. Every day at work would be different - a big fire, a crash on the motorway or looking for a lost child. The only problem is, police officers and firefighters work at night and I like sleeping!

Jason, 14, London

---

8 Write

Write about a job you'd like to do.

I'd like to be an electrician because ...

Portfolio

9 Limerick

Go to page 94 and listen and complete the limerick.

TV in Britain

1 🎧 26 **Read**

Different rooms, different programmes

'We've got four TV sets in our house so quite often we have four different channels on at the same time – in different rooms of course. My sister's 16 and she's got her own widescreen TV in her room. I think she watches MTV all the time. She even watches it while she's doing her homework! She says it helps her to concentrate. I like watching films and quiz shows as well as wildlife programmes.'

Marie, 14, Manchester

Fifty Channels

'My mum and dad say that when they were our age they only had four channels. Four channels! How boring! These days we've got hundreds of channels but we only watch a few of them. I like watching the History Channel. The programmes about wars are really interesting. And my dad watches his favourite team, Chelsea, on the Sports Channel.

Sam, 13, London

TV Reality Shows

'All my family enjoys reality TV. We watch the programmes together and we talk about the people. My favourites are *Pop Idol* and *X Factor* – I think some of the bands and singers are really good. I never phone up to vote – it's too expensive.'

Sadie, 13, Plymouth

Documentaries and Soaps

'I'd rather watch BBC programmes because they never have adverts. The adverts on the other channels are so boring! The BBC also has good documentaries and a programme about cars called *Top Gear*. That's really cool.

The only programmes I always watch are a couple of soaps. One is *EastEnders*. All my friends watch it too and we talk about it non-stop at school. I also watch an Australian soap called *Neighbours*. It's very different from *EastEnders* because the sun's always shining and most of the characters are really good-looking young people.'

Nick, 14, Liverpool

FACT FILE
- British teenagers watch TV four hours a day or 28 hours a week (on average).
- 77% of them have got a TV in their room.
- Teenagers with TVs in their bedrooms do less well at school.
- 74% of British homes now have satellite or cable TV.

2 Check

a) Read about the people and match the two parts of the sentences.

1 e)

1 There are four TV sets	a) reality TV shows.
2 Marie's sister watches TV	b) his favourite soaps.
3 Sam's family can watch	c) for her favourite singers.
4 Sam's dad is	d) while she's doing her homework.
5 Sadie likes watching	e) in Marie's house.
6 Sadie doesn't vote	f) the adverts on TV.
7 Nick doesn't like	g) a Chelsea fan.
8 He always watches	h) fifty different channels.

b) Read the fact file and answer right (✓) or wrong (✗).

1 British teenagers watch a lot of TV. ✓
2 13% of British teenagers don't have a TV in their room.
3 Teenagers without a TV in their room do less well at school.
4 Only 26% of British homes now have satellite or cable TV.
5 BBC 1 is a TV channel.

3 🎧 Listen

Listen and complete Anusha's answers to a TV survey.

TV Survey

1 How often do you watch TV?
2 When do you watch?
3 What sort of programmes do you like watching?
4 What's your favourite TV series?
5 Where do you sit when you watch TV?
6 How often do you watch a DVD?

4 Speak

a) Talk about your TV viewing habits. Use the questions in Exercise 3 to help you.

A: *How often do you watch TV?*
B: *I watch TV for an hour every day.*

b) Tell the class about your partner.

Andreas watches TV for an hour every day.

Project

Portfolio

My favourite TV programmes

Writing tip

Linkers: *too, also, as well as*

When we want to add information, we can use *too, also* and *as well as*.

1 *Too* comes at the end of the sentence.
   *My sister likes soaps. I like them **too**.*
2 *Also* often comes after the verb *to be* but before the main verb.
   *EastEnders is a soap. Neighbours **is also** a soap.*
   *My brother watches EastEnders. He **also** watches Neighbours.*
3 *As well as* comes before a noun.
   ***As well as** soaps, I like wildlife programmes.*
   *I like wildlife programmes **as well as** soaps.*

Find examples of *too, also* and *as well as* in Exercise 1.

Write about your favourite programmes.

My favourite programmes

My favourite programme is a soap called … . It's about … .
I like it because … .
As well as that soap, I like watching … .

25 Revision

1 Correct the spelling of the computer words in CAPITALS.

1 You can send or receive an email.

1   You can NEDS or CEREIVE an email.
    Send   receive

2   When you're on your computer, you look at a TROMION or a CERENS.
    monitor   screen

3   You can download SUMIC or WOSATFER from the Internet.
    music   software

4   You can surf the BEW or the TENTRINE.
    Web   Internet

5   You have to PONE and then CHIWTS NO a laptop before you can use it.
    open   switch on

6   You can write a XETT SAMSEGE on your mobile or an LIEMA on your PC.
    Text message   email

7   When you're surfing the net, you can click on an NOCI or a SEWBITE.
    Icon   website

8   Every laptop has a BEYOKARD and a ROMEMY.
    keyboard   memory

2 Complete this discussion about the future with *'ll, will* or *won't.*

Teacher: Can you tell me what ¹*will* be different in the year 3000?

Student A: The world's climate ²... be different. It ³... be much warmer.

Student B: Cars ⁴... use petrol or oil. They ⁵... use electricity instead.

Student C: The world ⁶... be much more crowded.

Teacher: And what ⁷... happen as a result of that?

Student C: A lot of people ⁸... go and live on the moon.

Student A: No, they ⁹... . There's no air on the moon.

Student B: We ¹⁰... have teachers in the future, only computers. So, I'm sorry, but you ¹¹... have a job!

Teacher: Ah, but that's not a problem because I ¹²... be here in the year 3000!

3 🎧 **Sounds fun:** Elision /t/ + /t/, /g/ and /f/

Listen, then listen and repeat.

Don't take long – I won't take long!
Don't go mad – I won't go mad!
Don't forget the time –
I won't forget the time!
I'll come back soon, so don't be sad.

4 Complete the crossword with verbs about getting ready for a party.

Across
1   We must *b u y* things to eat and drink.
2   So we must _ _ _ _ _ _ some money.
3   I'll _ _ _ _ the sandwiches.
4   And I'll _ _ _ the cloth on the table.

Down
5   We must _ _ _ _ some of this furniture.
6   I'll _ _ _ _ out the music.
7   And I'll _ _ _ _ _ _ the balloons.

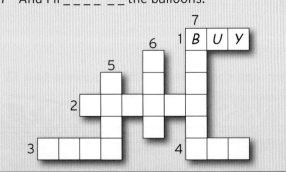

5 Match the words with the furniture in the pictu[re]

1 armchair

• cupboard • sofa • mirror • armchair • bookcase
• curtains • rug • chair • lamp • desk • carpet

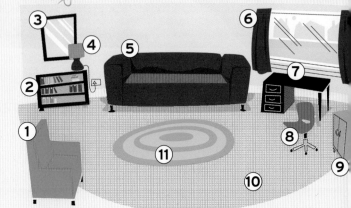

6 Complete with *will, 'll* or *won't*.

Jess: I can't do my Maths homework. ¹*Will* you help me?

Rose: Yes, of course I ²... . I ³... have my supper and then I ⁴... come over after that.

Jess: ⁵... you be long?

Rose: No, I promise I ⁶... . I ⁷... come to your house in about an hour.

Jess: ⁸... you bring your calculator? I can't find mine.

Rose: Yes, I⁹... bring my calculator. Now stop worrying.

7 <u>Underline</u> the right alternative.

Sam: What ¹*would you like/do you like* to do? ²*You like/Would you like* to go bowling?

Matt: No, ³*I'd prefer/I'm preferring* to go skating.

Chloe: ⁴*I'd rather/I rather* go swimming.

Katy: And ⁵*I'm liking/I'd like to* go to the cinema. How about you, Ruth? What ⁶*would you prefer/would you rather* do?

Ruth: ⁷*I'd like to do/I'd like doing* what you all want to do.

Sam: But that's the problem. ⁸*We'd all like doing/ We'd all like to do* different things!

8 Who's talking? Choose from:

- a police officer • a carpenter • an electrician
- a vet • a TV newsreader • a ski instructor
- a detective • a hairdresser • a journalist
- a firefighter • a plumber • a pilot
- a computer engineer

1 'The President of the USA is coming to Britain next week.'
TV newsreader

2 'How old is your cat, Mrs White?'

3 'Where were you at the time of the murder?'

4 'Where do you want the bath and toilet?'

5 'It's too hot and it's too dangerous.'

6 'We are landing at Heathrow Airport in ten minutes.'

7 'I'm going to put more memory into this PC.'

9 🔊 Chat time

a) You are planning a party. In pairs, follow the cues and write a conversation. Then act it out.

A: *Don't forget I'm having a party on Saturday.*
B: *I won't forget, I promise. I'll bring some food or drink.*

Student A   **Student B**

Tell Student B not to forget that you are having a party on Saturday.

> Say you won't forget. Say you'll bring some food or drink.

Thank Student B and ask which he/she would rather bring, food or drink.

> Say which you'd prefer to bring.

Remind Student B to bring his/her CD player.

> Promise you won't forget.

b) Listen to Jake and Ollie and compare your conversation.

10 A crazy party

Write the correct furniture words.

1 wardrobe

When I went to Jess and Ollie's party, there were a lot of people there. I hung my coat in a ¹ARMCHAIR upstairs in Ollie's bedroom. A girl was standing in front of the ²CARPET brushing her hair. In the sitting room the ³CHAIRS were closed but no one had switched on any ⁴MIRRORS so there wasn't much light. Three people were sitting on a ⁵WARDROBE. Ollie was sitting in an ⁶CUPBOARD. Next to him, sitting on two ⁷LAMPS, were two of his friends. Other people were sitting on the ⁸CURTAINS on the floor. Jake had found a lot of CDs in a ⁹SOFA.

What can you do?

I can:
- ask and talk about future predictions ☐
- offer to do things ☐
- talk about my ambitions ☐
- ask and talk about jobs I would like to do ☐

26 If something goes wrong, ...

Letter Page

Have you got a problem?
Tell us about it! Maybe we can help.

Problem brother!

Dear Harriet,

I've got a six-year-old brother, Rory, who gets on my nerves. He's really annoying. If I'm on my mobile, he turns up the volume on the TV so I can't hear. If I shout at him, my mum says, 'What's the matter with you today? You're in a bad mood!' or 'You're very bad-tempered!'

My mum and dad are easy-going with my brother all the time. If he wants a new game, he always gets it, but if I want something like new trainers, Mum says: 'Do you really need them?' And another thing, he stays up until at least nine o'clock every night. When I was his age, they were really strict about my bedtime. It's just not fair.

Max (14)

Harriet replies:

I completely understand. Younger brothers and sisters can be really annoying but on the whole your little brother sounds fairly normal! The sensible way is to be nice to him. The next time he annoys you, try to be patient. He probably just wants your attention. Why not try to spend some more time with him? Perhaps you could play a computer game together before you do your homework? But make sure you let him win occasionally!

Now listen and repeat Max's problem.

Everyday phrases

- He gets on my nerves.
- [You're] in a bad mood [today]!
- ... all the time.
- [Until] at least [nine o'clock].
- On the whole [he sounds fairly normal]!

2 Check

Answer the questions.

1 Who is Rory?
   He's Max's brother.
2 What does Rory do when his brother is on the phone?
3 What time does Rory go to bed?
4 What do Rory's parents always buy him?
5 Does Harriet think he sounds normal?

26

Look and learn

Zero conditional

If I'm on my mobile, **he turns up** the TV.
If he wants something new, **he** always **gets** it.

3 Speak

a) Make five sentences.

1   *If I'm on my mobile, he turns up the TV.*

Situation	Result
1 If I (be) on my mobile,	a) Mum (ask) if I really need them.
2 If I (shout) at him,	b) he (turn up) the TV.
3 If he (want) a new game,	c) my mum (say) I'm in a bad mood.
4 If I (want) some new trainers,	d) he always (get) it.

b) Work with a friend. Ask and answer about what happens to you in these situations.

A: *What happens if you get a phone call?*
B: *If I get a phone call, my mum wants to know who phoned me.*

1   You get a phone call.
2   You want a new pair of jeans.
3   You shout at your brother/sister.
4   You want to stay up.
5   Your room is untidy.

4 🎧 Memory check: Personality adjectives 1

Find the eight adjectives in this wordsnake. Then listen and check.

1 friendly

FRIENDLY POLITE RUDE SHY CLEVER HELPFUL LAZY FUNNY

5 🎧 New words: Personality adjectives 2

Listen and repeat.

• loyal • greedy • sensible • moody • honest
• dishonest • patient • impatient • annoying
• bad-tempered • generous • mean • big-headed
• modest • easy-going • tidy • untidy

6 Speak

a) Describe the people in the pictures.

1   *He's generous.*

b) Discuss which adjectives in Exercise 5 you think are 'good' and which are 'bad'.

A: *I think loyal is good but greedy is bad.*
B: *I agree and I think moody is ... .*

7 🎧 Listen

Listen and complete the description of Zoe's personality.

My sister's name is Zoe. She's a bit ¹*big-headed* and sometimes she's quite ²... . She's also ³... . For example, she always takes the last slice of pizza. But she's also very ⁴... – she always tells the truth. She's very ⁵... too. She always gives me really cool birthday presents.

8 Write

Write a description of your own personality. Use the description of Zoe in Exercise 7 to help you.

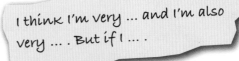

I think I'm very ... and I'm also very ... . But if I ... .

Portfolio

 # 27 If we put it under the grill ...

Recipe for *Party Pizza*

Ingredients (for four people)

1 ready-made pizza base

Tomato sauce
1 tablespoon of olive oil
1 onion (chopped)
400g tin of chopped tomatoes
Mixed herbs
Salt and black pepper

Toppings
Grated cheese
Mushrooms (sliced)
Black olives

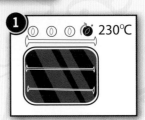

1 230°C
Heat the oven to 230°C.

2
Peel and chop the onion. If you peel onions under a tap, you won't cry!

3
Slice the mushrooms.

4
Heat the olive oil in a frying pan. Add the chopped onion with some salt and pepper and fry gently.

5
Add the tomatoes, herbs, salt and pepper and mix it all together.

6
Pour the tomato mixture into a saucepan and cook it for 10 minutes. It mustn't boil.

7
Spread the sauce over the pizza base.

8
Sprinkle with the grated cheese, mushrooms and olives.

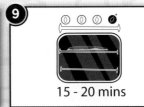

9 15 - 20 mins
Put the pizza in the oven and bake for 15-20 minutes.

10
When it is ready and the cheese has melted, serve immediately.

1 (2 34) Read

Read the recipe. Then listen and repeat the instructions.

2 Check

Correct the sentences.

1 The pizza is big enough for ~~six~~ people.
   Four
2 They must heat the oven to 220°C.
3 They must heat the olive oil in a saucepan.
4 The tomato mixture must boil.
5 Put the pizza in the frying pan for 15-20 minutes.

3 (2 35) Memory check: Food and drink

a) Complete these food and drink words with *a, e, i, o* or *u*. Then listen and repeat.

bre_a_d   m_lk   b_n_n_   b_sc__t   b_tt_r   ch__s_   cr__m
h_n_y   s__s_g_   s_g_r   ch_ck_n   p_st_   t_m_t_   c_rr_t
j_m   p_t_t_   r_c_

b) Can you think of any more food and drink words? You can add words from Exercise 1.

4 (2 36) New words: Cooking verbs

Listen and repeat. Which verbs are not in Exercise 1?

• cook • peel • slice • chop • mix • beat • pour • heat • melt
• bake • boil • fry • burn • taste • sprinkle • serve • grill

5 🎧 ²/₃₇ Read and listen

Rose: I'm starving!

Jake: Mum says we can make a pizza.

Rose: But that'll take ages!

Jake: No! It won't take long if we use this ready-made pizza base. There's a recipe here in Mum's book. Look.

Rose: OK. It says 'chop the onion and slice the mushrooms.' Come on then!

Twenty minutes later

Rose: Right. If we put it under the grill, it'll cook faster.

Jake: Great. Let's go and watch *X Factor*.

Ten minutes later

Jake: I can smell burning!

Rose: Oh no! We forgot the pizza!

Now listen and repeat.

6 Check

Number the sentences in the correct order.

The pizza burns.	☐	Rose says she's hungry.	☐ 1
They look at a recipe.	☐	They put the pizza under the grill.	☐
They go and watch TV.	☐	They prepare the vegetables.	☐

Look and learn

First conditional (+ *will*)

If we put it under the grill, **it'll cook** faster.

If we don't use a recipe, the pizza **won't be** very nice.

Will we miss *X Factor* **if we make** a pizza first?

Think about language

In the *if* clause we use *the present simple/the will future*.

7 Speak

a) Use the prompts in A (with *if* + the present simple) and B (with future *will*) to talk about these situations.

1 *If you're hungry, we'll make a pizza.*

A
1 you/be/hungry,
2 we/follow/Mum's recipe
3 we/use/this pizza base,
4 we/put/it under the grill,
5 we/not remember/it,

B
1 we/make/a pizza.
2 it/be/easy.
3 it/not take/long.
4 it/cook/faster.
5 it/burn.

b) In pairs, ask and answer.

A: *What will happen if we follow Mum's recipe?*

B: *It will be easy.*

8 Write

Portfolio

Write a recipe for a class collection of favourite recipes. Use the recipe in Exercise 1 as a model.

9 🎧 ²/₃₈ Limerick

Go to page 94 and listen and complete the limerick.

Come and watch as we feed the fish!

Daily schedule:
11.30 Sting ray talk and feed
2.00p.m. Shark talk
2.30p.m. Shark feed

1 Listen and read

The friends are visiting the London Aquarium.

Rose: Gosh, it's hot! I'm baking. I'm going to take off my jacket. Jake, can I put it in your backpack?

Jake: Yeah, if there's room.

Ollie: Look. They're feeding the sharks at 2p.m. We may be just in time. Come on.

Later

Jess: Excuse me, is it all right if I take a photo of the sharks?

Girl: Yes, sure. Don't forget to turn off the flash.

Ollie: There's one! It's huge. Quick, Jess. Take a photo!

Jess: No, not yet. I'm not ready. I'll take one when it comes round again.

Girl: Watch carefully. It'll be very excited when it sees the food.

Ollie: Here it comes, Jess. Get ready!

Jake: Be careful! It may jump out of the tank and bite you!

Jess: Very funny!

Now listen and repeat.

Everyday phrases

- Gosh, [it's hot]!
- I'm baking.
- Is it all right if I [take a photo]?
- There's one!
- No, not yet.
- Get ready!
- Be careful!

2 Check

Right (✓), wrong (✗) or don't know (DK)?

1 They feed the sting ray in the morning. ✓
2 Rose takes off her sweater.
3 She puts it in Ollie's backpack.
4 They feed the sharks three times a day.
5 Jess has got a camera.

3 New words: Phrasal verbs

a) Listen and repeat.

- turn on • turn off • put on • take off • get on
- get off • pick up • put down • throw away
- wake up

①

②

③

④

b) Match the verbs in a) to the pictures.

1 get on

Look and learn

Future time clause (+ *when*)
I'll take a photo **when the shark comes round**.
It'll be very excited **when it sees** the food.

Think about language
In the *when* clause we use *the present simple/the will future*.

---

4 Speak

Use the prompts to make sentences.

She'll take a photo when she sees the shark.

1 She/take/a photo/when/she/see/the shark.
2 The shark/be/excited when it/see/the food.
3 They/leave/the London Aquarium/when it/close.
4 Rose/put/her jacket/on/when they/leave.
5 They/look at/Jess's photos when/they/be on the bus.
6 They/have/supper when they/get/home.

5 English in action: Asking permission

a) Listen. Then practise the dialogue.

A: *Is it all right if I take a photo?*
B: *Yes, sure./Yes, it's fine./Yes, no problem.*
A: *Thanks. And can I use a flash?*
B: *No, I'm sorry. I'm afraid you can't.*

b) Act similar conversations, using these cues.

1 take off my jacket/put it in your backpack
2 borrow your camera/download the photos on my laptop
3 use your laptop/send an email
4 watch this DVD/take it home with me

c) Ask permission to do things at a friend's house.

Look and learn

Modal: *may*
We **may** be in time.
It **may** jump out.

---

6 Write

Rewrite the sentences with *may*.

1 It's possible I'll be late.
   I may be late.
2 It's possible she'll come this afternoon.
3 Perhaps it'll rain tomorrow.
4 Perhaps her mobile is switched off.
5 It's possible we'll go to the cinema.
6 It's possible I'll buy a new mobile phone.

7 Listen

Listen and complete the sentences.

1 The school holiday starts on *Friday*.
2 Rose's parents are going to … .
3 Ollie is playing in a … match.
4 Rose wants Jess to come at … .
5 They'll eat a … .

8 Joke

Q: What did the Egyptian Pharaoh say when he had a nightmare?
A: 'I want my mummy!'

How do you use your computer?

I use my computer to play games. I've got about twenty games and I play online with my friends and people from all over the world. Apart from games, I use my computer to keep in touch with my cousins in Australia and my penfriend Luis in Spain. I used to send emails to them but now I prefer to chat to them using Skype. We can see each other on our webcams so it's much better than a normal phone.

Lee, 14

I use my computer to surf the net and search for information on lots of different websites when I'm doing homework. I also use Wikipedia a lot. It's always up-to-date although it's not 100% correct so I check the facts. I use Word to write my essays and I insert images using Clip Art so they look really good. There's one more thing I've learnt. I now save everything because I once lost a long essay when my computer crashed.

Susie, 13

Leon, 14

I use my computer to download songs from the Internet. When I hear some music I like on the radio, I log onto iTunes and download it onto my MP3 player. Now I've got over 800 songs. I also download different ring tones for my mobile. I've got a really cool one at the moment – it's the music from *Superman*.

I live on a farm in Scotland and I mainly use my computer for instant messaging. Most evenings I'm on my computer and I'm 'talking' to my friends and cousins who live all over the country. I also write a blog about my life in a small farming community. My blog puts me in touch with other teenagers who live on farms and we can share experiences.

Shona, 13

1 ⟨2/43⟩ Read and check

a) Write a list of ten things you can do with a computer.

You can search for information.

b) Read the text. Tick (✓) the things you had on your list.

New words
- up-to-date • insert images • crash (*v*)
- online • keep in touch • Skype • webcam
- instant messaging • blog • share experiences
- log onto • ring tones

Study tip

How to improve your speaking

- Speak English as often as possible.
- Don't be shy. Speak clearly. Emphasise the important words, e.g. nouns, verbs, adjectives and adverbs.
- Don't be afraid to make mistakes.
- Practise reading dialogues aloud when you are alone.
- Listen to other people speaking English.
- Before a discussion, make notes to help you.

Remember these things when you speak in Exercise 2.

2 Speak

a) In pairs or groups, discuss the following statement. Use the phrases below in your discussion.

Computers aren't always a good thing.

I agree.

You're right.

That's true.

I'm not sure.

I don't (really) agree.

A: *I don't agree. Computers are fun and computer games are great.*
B: *That's true. But some people spend too much time on their computers instead of going out.*

b) Make a list of the points for and against computers.

For	Against
fun	too much time

c) Tell the class.

We agree that computers aren't always a good thing. One problem is that some people spend too much time on them.

3 🎧 Listen

Listen to Jess explaining to Rose how to use WordArt on her computer. She wants to make a cover for a school History project. Listen and complete the instructions. Use these words.

> • picture • image • print • toolbar • style
> • font • text • preview

1. Click 'Insert' on the Word *toolbar.* .
2. Now click ... and then click WordArt.
3. Choose the WordArt ... you want.
4. Write the title of your project in the ... box.
5. Now choose the ... style and size you want.
6. Change the ... size by clicking on the title and dragging the border.
7. Choose Print ... on your toolbar.
8. Check that it's OK and then click ... .

The Fire of London

Project

Portfolio

People and their computers

Choose three people from this list. Write about how they use computers in their jobs.

- A student
- A teacher
- A journalist
- A pilot
- An astronaut
- A vet

A student uses a computer to find facts and information about the subject which he/she is studying.

30 Revision

1 **Complete the sentences with the verbs in the present simple.**

1 If Rose *has* (have) a Maths test, she ... (worry) about it.
2 If Jess ... (argue) with a friend, she ... (talk) to Rose.
3 If Ollie... (invite) his friends home, Jess always ... (talk) to them.
4 Ollie ... (be) in a bad mood for days if he ... (lose) a basketball match.
5 If Rory ... (get) a phone call at home, Max ... (not listen).
6 Jake ... (not buy) clothes if his sister ... (not like) them.

2 **What personality adjectives describe these people?**

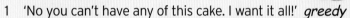

• bad-tempered • loyal • patient • big-headed
• honest • greedy • generous • sensible

1 'No you can't have any of this cake. I want it all!' *greedy*
2 'I'm good at basketball and football. And I'm clever as well.'
3 'Of course you can borrow my mobile. Talk for as long as you like.'
4 'Oh, go away. I don't want to talk to you.'
5 'It's all right. I don't mind waiting. Take your time.'
6 'I never cycle without my helmet on.'
7 'I don't like it when you say bad things about one of my friends.'
8 'I found a wallet with a lot of money in it yesterday. I took it to the police.'

3 **Cross out the incorrect verb.**

You can ...

1 ... peel/chop/~~beat~~ an onion.
2 ... fry/sprinkle/ boil an egg.
3 ... melt/slice/ bake a potato.
4 ... heat/pour/ grill a sauce.
5 ... cook/sprinkle/ burn a pizza.
6 ... heat/taste/serve an ice cream.

4  **Sounds fun /ɔɪ/**

Listen, then listen and repeat.

Toyah's little boy Roy
Has dropped his toy
In some oil!

5 **Jake and Ollie are arranging a trip to the beach. Complete the conversation with the correct form of the verb in brackets.**

Jake: If it ¹*is* (be) fine tomorrow we ²*'ll go* (go) to the beach.

Ollie: OK, if you ³... (come) to my house at about nine o'clock, we ⁴... (leave) at 9.30.

Jake: If we ⁵... (have) a big breakfast we ⁶... (not be) hungry till about two.

Ollie: But we must take something to eat. I ⁷... (make) the sandwiches if you ⁸... (bring) the drinks.

Jake: If the girls ⁹... (want) to come, we ¹⁰... (let) them.

Ollie: Yes, of course. And we ¹¹... (play) football on the beach if you ¹²... (bring) a ball.

Jake: OK, but if it ¹³... (rain) tomorrow, we ¹⁴... (not go).

30

6 Complete the sentences with the correct phrasal verbs from the box.

- pick up • turn on • take off • throw away
- get off • put down • get on • put on
- wake up • turn off

1 It'll be difficult to *get on* the bus with all these bags.
2 ... the television. There's a programme I want to watch.
3 I'm going to ... another sweater. It's cold in here.
4 Don't ... that bag. We may need it.
5 ... those clothes. Don't leave them on the floor like that.
6 We'll ... at the next bus stop. We can walk from there.
7 ... your dirty boots before you come in the house.
8 ...! It's 7.30 and breakfast's ready.
9 ... that book. I want to talk to you.
10 ... the light. I want to go to sleep.

7 Correct the mistakes.

1 I'll phone you when I will arrive.
   I'll phone you when I arrive.
2 Send me a text message when you will get home.
3 When she'll know the answer, she'll tell you.
4 When the bus will stop, we'll all get off.
5 I'll go to bed when this programme will finish.
6 When it'll stop raining, we'll go for a walk.

8 Look at the things the friends are going to take with them when they go cycling. Write sentences with *may* or *may not*.

1 *They're going to take sweaters.*
   It may be cold.

1 sweaters/be cold
a tent/not find a hostel
a mobile/phone home
4 some water/be hot
5 raincoats/rain
6 swimsuits/go swimming
7 some money/buy some food
8 a map/not remember the way home

9 🔊 2 46 Chat time

a) You are at a friend's house. In pairs, follow the cues and write a conversation. Then act it out.

A: *Is it all right if I use your mobile? I want to phone home.*
B: *No, I'm sorry. It needs recharging.*

Student A	Student B

Ask Student B's permission to use her mobile. You want to phone home.

Apologise. Say that it needs recharging. Say you'll recharge it now.

Ask how long it takes to recharge her mobile.

Say you are not sure. It may be half an hour.

Thank Student B. Ask if you can play a game on her laptop while you are waiting.

Agree. Say it's no problem.

b) Listen to Jess and Rose talking and compare your conversation.

10 Puzzle: Missing foods

Complete the words.

1 peel
a p *o t a t* o
a b _ _ _ _ a

2 melt
b _ _ _ _ r
c _ _ _ _ e

3 pour
s _ _ _ e
o _ l

4 bake
b _ _ _ d
a c _ _ e

5 fry
an e _ g
a s _ _ _ _ _ e

6 slice
a t _ _ _ _ o
an o _ _ _ n

What can you do?

I can:

- describe people ☐
- ask and talk about situations with *if* and *will* ☐
- ask and talk about situations with *when* and *will* ☐
- ask permission to do things ☐

31 We have to pay ...

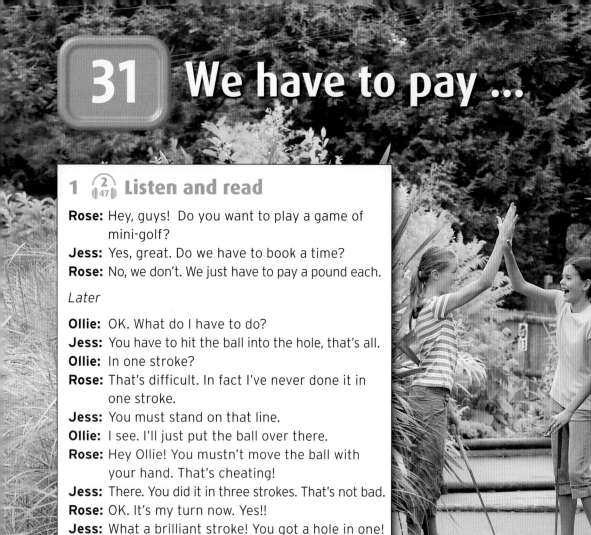

1 🎧 2/47 Listen and read

Rose: Hey, guys! Do you want to play a game of mini-golf?

Jess: Yes, great. Do we have to book a time?

Rose: No, we don't. We just have to pay a pound each.

Later

Ollie: OK. What do I have to do?

Jess: You have to hit the ball into the hole, that's all.

Ollie: In one stroke?

Rose: That's difficult. In fact I've never done it in one stroke.

Jess: You must stand on that line.

Ollie: I see. I'll just put the ball over there.

Rose: Hey Ollie! You mustn't move the ball with your hand. That's cheating!

Jess: There. You did it in three strokes. That's not bad.

Rose: OK. It's my turn now. Yes!!

Jess: What a brilliant stroke! You got a hole in one!

Now listen and repeat.

Everyday phrases

- ... that's all.
- In fact [I've never done it in one stroke].
- I see.
- That's cheating!
- That's not bad.
- It's my turn now.
- What a [brilliant stroke]!

2 🎧 2/48 New words: Sports places

a) Listen and repeat.

- course - court - park - pitch - pool - ring
- rink - track

b) Match the sports with the places.

1 football pitch

1 football 2 tennis 3 athletics 4 golf
5 swimming 6 boxing 7 ice skating 8 skateboarding

3 Check

Who ...	Rose	Jess	Ollie
1 suggests they play mini-golf?	✓		
2 knows how much it costs?			
3 tells Ollie what to do?			
4 hits the ball first?			
5 does it in three strokes?			
6 gets a hole in one?			

31

Look and learn

Modals: *must/mustn't/have to* (obligation and prohibition)

must

Positive
You **must** stand on that line.

Negative
You **mustn't** move the ball.

have to

Positive
You **have to** hit the ball.

Negative
You **don't have to** book a time.

Question
What do I **have to** do?

Think about language
What's the difference?
You *don't have to* play on Sunday.
You *mustn't* play on Sunday.

4 Write

Jess is teaching Ollie how to play mini-golf. Complete their conversation.

Mini-golf course

Rules
- Booking isn't necessary
- Special clothes aren't needed
- Pay before you play
- Always start at the 1st hole
- The course closes at 6p.m.

Ollie: ¹*Do we have to* book a time?

Jess: No, we don't. We just ²... pay a pound.

Ollie: Do I ³... wear special clothes?

Jess: No, you ⁴... . You can wear what you like.

That afternoon

Ollie: There are lots of people. Let's start at hole 4.

Man: Excuse me! You ⁵... start there! You ⁶... start at the first hole.

Ollie: I'm sorry.

Jess: Come on, Ollie. We ⁷... play one game before six o'clock!

5 Speak

a) Work in pairs. Talk about the things you have to do during school term time and during school holidays.

1 **A:** *What time do you have to get up during term time?*
  B: *I have to get up at 7.15. What about you?*

1 What time/get up/during term time?
2 What time/leave/home/term time?
3 How much homework/do/term time?
4 Write projects/school holidays?
5 What time/go to bed/term time/school holidays?

b) Tell the class about your friend.

6 Listen

Listen and complete the rules of volleyball.

Volleyball equipment and rules

1 You must have a big .*ball*. and a net.
2 You play on a ... .
3 You can play ... or outdoors.
4 The court is ... long and nine metres wide.
5 There are ... players in each team.
6 You usually hit the ball with your ... or arms but you don't have to. You can use any part of your body.
7 Players on the same team can only hit the ball ... times.
8 One team scores a ... if the ball hits the ground.

7 Write

Choose a different sport and describe it in the same way as in Exercise 6. Use the words *must*, *mustn't*, *have to* and *don't have to* in your description.

Handball
To play handball you must have two teams of ... .

8 Did you know?

The modern sport of tennis started in 1874. A British army officer, Major Walter Wingfield, invented and patented the game. The only difference was his court was shaped like an 8. Rich people with large gardens played the game on their lawns. Then the game quickly became very popular in Britain and the USA.

2 🎧 (3/03) Listen and read

Jake is going to do a 'Fun Run' in the park.

Rose: Morning, Mum. Have you got an aspirin?

Mum: Yes. What's the matter with you?

Rose: I've got a headache and a sore throat.
I think I'm getting a cold.

Mum: Have you got a temperature?

Rose: I don't know.

Jake: You're not ill! It's because you always
sleep with your window shut. You should
sleep with it open.

Rose: Bossy boots! Are you ready for your run?

Jake: Yes - in my new trainers!

Rose: You shouldn't wear new trainers for a run.

Mum: Rose's right. You should wear your
comfortable old trainers, Jake.
Just to be sure.

Jake: My new ones are fine and I like them!

Mum: OK, but I'm a bit worried.

Three hours later

Mum: Well done!

Jake: Oooh! I've got a blister on my heel.

Rose: That's because you wore your new
trainers!

Now listen and repeat.

1 🎧 (3/02) New words: Common illnesses

**Listen and repeat. Then write the names of
the illnesses under the pictures.**

• a cold • a cough • a sore throat • a headache
• a stomachache • a temperature

1 *a cough* 2 .... 3 ....

4 .... 5 .... 6 ....

Everyday phrases

▪ What's the matter [with you]?
▪ [Rose]'s right.
▪ Just to be sure.
▪ I'm a bit [worried].
▪ Well done!

3 Check

Match the two parts of the sentences.

1 f)

1 Rose has got	a) an aspirin.
2 She wants	b) his new trainers.
3 She sleeps	c) a fun run.
4 Jake is going to do	d) with a blister.
5 He's wearing	e) with her window shut.
6 He comes back	f) a headache.

> **Look and learn**
>
> **Talking about illness**
>
> What's the matter with you?
> I've got a headache/a cold.
> What's the matter with him/her?
> He's/She's got a headache/a cold.

4 Speak and act

a) Ask and answer about the people in Exercise 1.

1 **A:** *What's the matter with him?*
 B: *He's got a cough.*

b) Work in pairs. One of you acts an illness, the other guesses what it is.

A: *What's the matter with me?*
B: *You've got a stomachache.*

> **Look and learn**
>
> **Modal: *should/shouldn't* (advice)**
>
> You **should** sleep with your window open.
> You **shouldn't** wear your new trainers.

5 Speak

Work in pairs. Give advice with *should* and *shouldn't*.

A: *What's the matter with you?*
B: *I've got a temperature.*
A: *Well, you shouldn't go out.*
 You should go to bed.

Illness	Advice
A temperature	→ not go out/go to bed
A stomachache	→ lie down/not eat a curry
A cough	→ not go to school/take cough medicine
A headache	→ take an aspirin/not listen to loud music
A sore throat	→ take some throat tablets/not go to a party

6 🎧 English in action: Visiting a doctor

a) Listen. Then practise the conversation.

A: *Good morning. Now, what's the matter with you?*
B: *I've got a sore throat, Dr Jones. I've had it for a week.*
A: *I see. I'll give you some medicine but you should stay at home for a day or two.*
B: *Thank you.*
A: *Come back and see me if you don't feel better next week.*

b) Act more conversations with a doctor. Use the prompts.

1 **A:** a temperature/two days
 B: some tablets/drink a lot of water and go to bed
2 **A:** a cough and a bad cold/a week
 B: some medicine/not go to school for a few days

7 🎧 Listen

Listen to a conversation between Kate and her mum. Are the statements right (✓) or wrong (✗)?

1 There's nothing wrong with Kate. ✗
2 Her mum feels her head.
3 Her temperature is 39°.
4 Kate wants to go to bed.
5 Her mum doesn't want her to go to a party.

8 Write

Write an answer to the problem below. Use these prompts to help you.

- not worry
- drink a lot of water
- not eat a lot of fat or sugar
- wash your face three times a day
- see your doctor

You shouldn't worry ...

I've got a lot of spots on my face.
I've had them for a year now.
They look horrible. What should I do?

Sam, 14, Bournemouth

33 What would you do?

How brave are you?

What would you do in these situations?

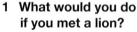

1 What would you do if you met a lion?
a) I'd faint.
b) I'd run away.
c) I'd stand very still.

2 What would you do if you saw a mouse in your bedroom?
a) I'd chase it.
b) I'd hide under the bedclothes.
c) I'd call for my mum or dad.

3 What would you do if you bro[ke] your mother's favourite vase?
a) I'd hide all the pieces.
b) I'd tell her immediately.
c) I'd try to mend the vase.

5 What would you do if you heard a strange noise at night?
a) I'd shout 'Who is it?'
b) I'd tell my parents.
c) I'd be afraid and cry.

4 What would you do if your teacher asked you to make a speech to the school?
a) I'd say: 'Please ask another student.'
b) I wouldn't come to school that day.
c) I'd do it.

UUUHHHH

How did you do?

If you answered 1c 2a 3b 4c 5a: You're probably very brave. But don't forget, being brave isn't always sensible!

If you answered 1b 2c 3c 4a 5b: You're quite brave but you're also quite sensible. Sometimes you'd like to be a bit braver. Why not try?

If you answered 1a 2b 3a 4b 5c: You need someone to protect you. You aren't brave at all but you're probably a very nice person.

1  Read

Read the magazine quiz. Then listen and repeat the quiz questions.

2 Check

Do the quiz in pairs. Read out the questions and note your partner's answers. Then read the score results.

3 Write

Complete the conversation using the second conditional, then act the conversation.

A: What ¹*would you do* (you/do) if you ²... (see) a mouse in your bedroom?

B: I ³... (jump) on my bed.

A: And then what ⁴... (you/do)?

B: I ⁵... (wait) for someone to come.

A: But if there ⁶... (not/be) anyone in the house, ⁷... (you wait) for someone to come home?

B: No, I ⁸... , I ⁹... (ring) you on my mobile.

A: But if you ¹⁰... (ring) me, I ¹¹... (not help) you. I'm even more scared of mice than you are!

4 Speak

What would you do in these situations? Ask and answer in groups.

1 **A:** *What would you do if you were lost in a forest?*
  B: *I would try to go back the way I came in.*
  C: *I would stay where I was and wait for someone to find me.*

1 You are lost in a forest.
2 You are cycling and you see a forest fire coming towards you.
3 You are on a boat and a friend who can't swim falls into the water.
4 You are walking with a friend when a snake bites her.
5 A dangerous dog starts to run after you.

5 New words: Adjectives with prepositions

Listen and repeat.

• mad about • good at • interested in • fond of
• keen on • proud of • scared of • bored with

6 Write

a) Complete the conversation with the correct adjective from Exercise 5.

Zoe: I'm ¹*bored* with skating. I'm not going to do it any more.

Mel: But why? You used to be ²... about it. You practised every day.

Zoe: Yes, I know I was ³... on it. I really enjoyed it. And I was ⁴... at it. I won a competition once, and my mum and dad were very ⁵... of me. But I'm just not so ⁶... in it any longer. And I've broken my leg once and I'm a bit ⁷... of breaking it again.

Mel: But what about all your skating friends?

Zoe: Yes, I'll miss them. I'm really ⁸... of them.

b) Now listen to Zoe and Mel and check your answers.

Look and learn

Second conditional (+ *might*)
If I saw a mouse in my bedroom I **might** scream or I **might** run out of the room.

---

7 Speak and write

a) Discuss these questions in pairs.

1 **A:** *Where would you go for your ideal holiday?*
  B: *I'm not sure. I think I might go to Disney World in Florida.*

1 Where would you go?
2 Who would you go with?
3 How would you travel?
4 Where would you stay?
5 What other places would you visit?
6 What things would you buy?

b) Write a description of your ideal holiday. Use the questions to help you.

8 Song: *Sweet Dreams My L.A. Ex* by Rachel Stevens

Go to page 94 and listen and join in the song.

Not old enough

James England had a part-time job as a newspaper boy. He was never late and he always delivered the right newspaper to the right house. But yesterday he lost his job. Why? Because he told the newsagent, Ken Halliday, it was his 12th birthday. 'He told me I wasn't old enough to have a part-time job,' said James. 'I'm very tall for my age so that's probably why he didn't ask me before.'

Mr Halliday, the newsagent, said, 'I thought he was 14 or 15 so I didn't ask for his age. James is a good worker so he can definitely have his job back next year – when he's 13.' James said, 'I'm really fed up because I enjoyed my job – and I enjoyed the money!'

What's the legal age?

AT ...	YOU CAN ...
AGE 11	• open a bank account
AGE 12	• buy a pet or an animal
AGE 13	• do a paid job for a few hours a week
AGE 14	• stay at home on your own without a babysitter
AGE 15	• see a Certificate 15 film at the cinema or on DVD
AGE 16	• leave school • leave home if your parents agree • get married if your parents agree • ride a moped up to 50cc • join the army • get a full-time job
AGE 17	• learn to drive a car • ride a motorbike between 50cc and 125cc • go to an adult prison • leave home even if your parents don't agree
AGE 18	• vote in an election • get married even if your parents don't agree • ride a motorbike above 125cc • own a house • get a tattoo • give blood • change your name

New words
- bank account • babysitter • army • full-time
- adult prison • election • own • tattoo • blood
- part-time • delivered • definitely • fed up

1 🎧 Read

a) Read about James England.

b) Read about young people and the law in the UK.

2 Check

a) Answer the questions about James England and his job.

1 How old was James yesterday?
   He was ...
2 What sort of shop does Ken Halliday have?
3 Why did he think James was older than he was?
4 How long must James wait before he can have his job back?
5 Would you like to have James's job? Why?/Why not?

b) Answer the questions about the legal ages with *Yes* or *No*.

1 Tom is 17. Can he ride a 250cc motorbike? *No*
2 Harriet is 16 and she wants to leave home. Can her parents stop her?
3 Kate is 14. Can her parents leave her at home without a babysitter?
4 Kevin is 16. Can he be sent to an adult prison?
5 Laura is 15. Can she leave school?

3 Speak

a) What are the legal ages in your country?

How old do you have to be to ...
1 ride a 50cc moped?
2 go to an adult prison?
3 get married?
4 drive a car?
5 vote in an election?
6 work part-time?

b) Work in pairs. Do you agree with these ages?

A: *I think the legal age to ride a moped is too old. What do you think?*

B: *I disagree. Mopeds are really dangerous ...*

4 🎧 Listen

Answer the questions.

1 How old is Nick now? *15*
2 When is his birthday?
3 What does his friend Tom want to sell?
4 How much does he want to sell it for?
5 How big is the engine?
6 How fast can it go?
7 Does Nick promise to wear a helmet?

Project

Legal ages in my country

Writing tip

Checking your work

When you finish your writing, you should give yourself time to check it.
Think about:

- grammar (e.g. Are you using the right verb tenses?)
- word order (e.g. Are the adjectives before, not after, the nouns?)
- spelling (Have you spelt all the words correctly?)
- punctuation (e.g. Do all your sentences start with a capital letter?)
- handwriting (Can someone read it? Are all the letters clear?)

When you finish writing your project, check your work carefully. Then ask a friend to check it too.

Write about the legal ages in your country. Find out how old you have to be to:

- get a part-time job
- leave school
- drive a moped, a motorbike or a car
- vote in an election
- join the army
- get married

In my country some legal ages are different from in the UK. For example, you have to be ... before you can get a part-time job. You have to be ... before ...

35 Revision

1 Complete the crossword with the places linked to the sports.

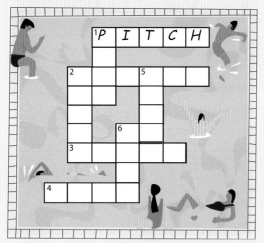

Crossword:
¹P I T C H

Across
1 football ...
2 golf ...
3 athletics ...
4 skating ...

Down
1 swimming ...
2 tennis ...
5 boxing ...
6 skateboard ...

2 <u>Underline</u> the correct alternative.

1 You *mustn't*/<u>*have to*</u> wear a helmet at a skateboard park.
2 You *must/mustn't* pay £5 to use this tennis court.
3 If you want to play tennis well, you *mustn't/must* have a good racket.
4 You *mustn't/don't have to* push people into the swimming pool. It's dangerous.
5 We *don't have to/mustn't* get out of the swimming pool at five. It doesn't close till seven o'clock.

3 Match the two sentences.

1 c)

1 My mum says I've got a temperature.
2 I've got a really bad headache.
3 I can't eat this toast.
4 Tom's only got a cold.
5 Ellie didn't sleep very well last night.
6 There was something wrong with that meat.

a) Can I have some aspirin?
b) I think he should go to school.
c) She says it's 42°.
d) I've got a terrible stomachache.
e) I've got a really sore throat.
f) Her cough kept her awake.

4 Complete the conversation with *should* or *shouldn't*.

Tom: Mum, I've got a really bad cold and I feel terrible.
Mum: Oh, poor you. You ¹*should* stay in bed. You ²... go to school today.
Tom: Do you think you ³... take my temperature? I feel very hot.
Mum: Yes, I think I ⁴... . Um, it's 39°. I think you ⁵... take two aspirin.
Tom: Do you think you ⁶... call a doctor?
Mum: No, I ⁷... worry too much, Tom. It's only a cold, not flu.

5 Rewrite the words of this conversation in the right order.

Doctor: the matter Good morning. with you? what's Now
Good morning. Now what's the matter with you?
Megan: a cough. I've got bad
Doctor: have you How long had it?
Megan: for a week. it I've had
Doctor: some medicine. OK, I'll you give for a day or two. to school go You shouldn't stay in bed. should You if you don't feel Come back in a few days. better
Megan: Doctor. much, very Thanks

35

6 Correct the mistakes in this conversation.

1 would you do

Kim: What ¹you would do if a teacher ²ask you to make a speech?

Zoe: I'm not sure what ³I do.

Amy: I think ⁴I will do it.

Beth: ⁵I'll say, 'Please ask another student.'

7 Sounds fun /aʊ/

Listen, then listen and repeat.

If you look out of the window now.
You'll see a brown cow
Walking around town
Mooing loudly!

Moo!

8 Complete the sentences with these prepositions.

| · in · about · of (x 3) · on · at · with |

1 I'm not scared *of* mice but I hate spiders.
2 I'm quite good ... basketball. It's my favourite sport.
3 I did well in my exams and my parents said they're proud ... me.
4 I'm bored ... this programme. Can we change channels?
5 My brother's mad ... computer games.
6 I'm keen ... Formula 1. I watch every race.
7 I'm not interested ... Chemistry. I prefer Biology.
8 I'm very fond ... my grandmother.

9 Chat time

a) In pairs, follow the cues and write a conversation. Then act it out.

Student A

Ask if Student B has ever entered a competition.

Ask Student B where he/she would go in the USA if he/she won.

Say where you'd go.

Say what you'd do there.
Say why.

Student B

Tell Student A you entered a competition last month and the prize is a holiday in the USA.

Say where you might go. Ask Student A where he/she would go.

Ask what he/she would do there?

Say you might do the same.

b) Listen to Jess and Rose and compare your conversation.

10 Puzzle

Read about the sports that these five friends are interested in. Complete the chart.

1 Abby is mad about volleyball and plays in her school team.
2 Ben used to be interested in volleyball but he was never very good at it and now he says he's bored with it.
3 Chloe is keen on the same sport as Abby.
4 Susie goes to the same tennis court every Saturday.
5 Ben is good at the same sport as his sister.
6 Danny isn't interested in volleyball or tennis but he goes to the local swimming pool three times a week.
7 Susie is Ben's sister.

	Tennis	Swimming	Volleyball
Abby			✓
Danny			
Chloe			
Susie			
Ben			

What can you do?

I can:

- ask and talk about things I have to do ☐
- ask and talk about illnesses ☐
- give advice ☐
- ask and talk about imaginary situations ☐

36 Is it really made of ice?

1 🎧 3/14 **Listen and read**

by Adam Newton

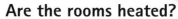

I DON'T BELIEVE IT!

Dan Barnes, 14, has just come back from Sweden, where he and his parents stayed in a hotel made of ice. Here's my interview with Dan.

Is the hotel really made of ice?
Yes it is. It's built in winter and in the summer it melts.

Is a new hotel built every year?
Yes. The main building is finished at the beginning of December. Then the sculptors arrive. The ice inside the hotel is carved to make furniture, doors and windows.

Is everything made of ice?
No, ice isn't used for everything. For example, the beds aren't made of ice, they're made of wood and the mattresses are made of foam rubber.

Is it very cold inside the hotel?
Well, the temperature inside the hotel is about five degrees below zero. Outside it can be forty degrees below zero! Inside the hotel I wore an anorak, moon boots and a woolly hat all the time!

Are the rooms heated?
No, they aren't, but special sleeping bags are provided by the hotel. They're made of synthetic fibre so they're very warm and people wear their hats in bed too!

Is there a restaurant?
Yes, you can get hot food and hot drinks. All the cold drinks are served in special ice glasses. The glass is made of ice so you have to wear gloves to hold it!

Does the hotel damage the environment?
I don't think so. The hotel is built from a natural materi – ice and it naturally recycles into water! The beds are used again each year. And, of course, the hotel doesn't use electricity for fridges!

Now listen and repeat the first four questions and answers.

2 Check

a) Right (✓), wrong (✗) or don't know (DK)?

1 Dan Barnes lives in Sweden. ✗
2 They build the hotel in the summer.
3 The sculptors start work in December.
4 The ice sculptors carve the beds.

5 It's warmer inside the hotel than outside.
6 Hotel guests wear their clothes in bed.
7 The hotel restaurant serves hot food.

b) Correct the wrong statements.

1 *Dan Barnes doesn't live in Sweden.*

36

Look and learn

Present simple passive

Positive
The hotel **is built** in winter.
The beds **are made** of wood.

Negative
Ice **isn't used** for everything.
The beds **aren't made** of ice.

Think about language
We make the passive with the verb *to be/to have* and the past participle.

3 Write

Rewrite the sentences in the passive.

1 The hotel is made of ice.

1   They make the hotel of ice.
2   Sculptors make the furniture.
3   They build the hotel in winter.
4   They finish the main building in December.
5   They don't make the beds of ice.
6   They don't heat the rooms.
7   The hotel provides special sleeping bags.

4 🎧 New words: Materials

a) Listen and repeat.

- leather   • glass   • wood   • metal
- cotton   • wool   • paper   • plastic
- rubber   • synthetic fibre

b) Match the object with the material.

1 glass

c) Talk about the objects and materials.

A: *What's a bottle made of?*
B: *It's usually made of glass or plastic.*

5 Speak

Work in groups. Ask and say what objects in the room are made of.

A: *What's this desk made of?*
B: *It's made of wood.*
     What are Marco's trainers made of?
C: *They're made of leather.*

6 🎧 Listen

Two friends, Luke and Sarah, are talking about the things they recycle. Complete the chart.

	Glass bottles	Plastic bottles	Clothes	Shoes	Paper	Tins	Drinks cans
Luke	✓	✗					
Sarah							

7 Write

Complete this letter to a teenage magazine about recycling. Use the verbs in brackets in the present simple, active or passive.

We ¹*are told* (tell) that we should ²... (recycle) everything. I agree, but I think the real problem is the supermarkets. Everything that ³... (sell) in supermarkets ⁴... (wrap) in a lot of plastic and paper. It's just not necessary. Also, every time we ⁵... (go) shopping, we ⁶... (give) lots of plastic bags by the supermarkets. We ⁷... (use) some of them again but in our family most of them ⁸... (throw away). I think that's terrible.

Katrina, 13, Cardiff

1 🎧 **3/17 Read**

On September 2nd 1666 in the City of London, a baker in Pudding Lane forgot to put out his oven fire before he went to bed. In the early morning, sparks from the oven fell onto some wood. Soon the baker's house was on fire. The fire spread through the city for five days. It was called the Great Fire of London.

The fire burned for a long time because the houses were built close together and they were made mainly of wood. The flames were seen for miles around, especially from the hills in the north of London. Luckily, strong winds stopped the fire from spreading south of the river. Eventually, gunpowder was used to blow up some of the buildings. This created firebreaks which, together with the river, stopped the flames from spreading.

Over two square kilometres of the city were destroyed in the fire; 13,200 houses and 87 churches (including St Paul's Cathedral) were burnt down. Thousands of people were left homeless and their lives were ruined by the Great Fire. Officially, only six people died because many managed to escape to the hills north of the city.

Today, the place of the baker's shop in Pudding Lane is marked by a tall column, the Monument.

A Prospect of LONDON as before the Fire

THAMESIS FLVVIVS.   South worke.

2 Check

Number the events in the correct order.

a) The fire destroyed a large area of the city. ☐
b) Sparks from the oven fell on to some wood. ☐
c) They built the Monument. ☐
d) A baker forgot to put out his oven fire. ☐ 1
e) They used gunpowder to blow up buildings. ☐
f) Strong winds stopped the fire from spreading. ☐

Look and learn

Past simple passive

Positive
It **was called** the Great Fire of London.
Thousands of houses **were destroyed** by the fire.

Negative
The fire **wasn't put out** by the baker.
Houses south of the river **weren't damaged** by the fire.

Think about language
We often use the preposition ... after the passive.

3 Speak

Work in pairs. Ask and answer the questions. Use the past simple passive.

1   **A:** *Who was the Great Fire of London started by?*
    B: *It was started by a baker.*

1   Who/the Great Fire of London/start/by?
2   What/the old houses/make/of?
3   How/firebreaks/create?
4   How many homes/destroy?
5   How many people/leave/homeless?
6   How many people/kill?

4 Read and write

Rewrite this description of the Monument in the present or past simple passive.

The Monument

The architect Christopher Wren designed the Monument. They built it between 1671 and 1677 to commemorate the Great Fire of London. They brought the stone for the Monument 300 kilometres from Portland, on the south coast of England. In the 17th century scientists also used it as a laboratory for experiments on gravity. In 1846 they put a roof on the balcony to stop people jumping off. If you climb the 311 steps to the top, they give you a certificate.

The Monument was designed by the architect Christopher Wren. It ...

5 🎧 New words: Buildings and landscape

Listen and repeat.

- church   • cathedral   • monument
- mountain   • ocean   • sea   • river
- forest   • desert   • lake   • coast
- valley   • hill   • stream   • island

6 Speak

a) Form two teams. Together think of an example of each of the following:

1 a mountain   2 a sea   3 an ocean
4 a river   5 a desert   6 a lake
7 an island   8 a monument

b) Ask the other team what they have thought of.

A: *What's the name of a mountain?*
B: *Mount Everest. What's the name of a sea?*

7 🎧 Listen

Listen to this description of the San Francisco earthquake and fire and answer the questions.

1   At what time was San Francisco hit by a huge earthquake?
2   What was the date?
3   How long did it last?
4   When was the fire put out?
5   What was the population of San Francisco?
6   Where were many people forced to live?
7   Officially, how many people were killed?
8   How many people were shot?

8 Did you know?

- San Francisco is built on the San Andreas Fault. Many earthquakes occur on this fault.
- The last big earthquake in the city was in 1989.
- There could be another huge earthquake at any time.

38 She says it's too late.

1 🎧 3/20 Listen and read

①
Jake: What's up, Jess? You look fed up.
Jess: I don't want to leave.
Ollie: Hey, do you want to come to the airport with us?
Rose: You bet. Is there room?
Ollie: Yes, the taxi's really big.

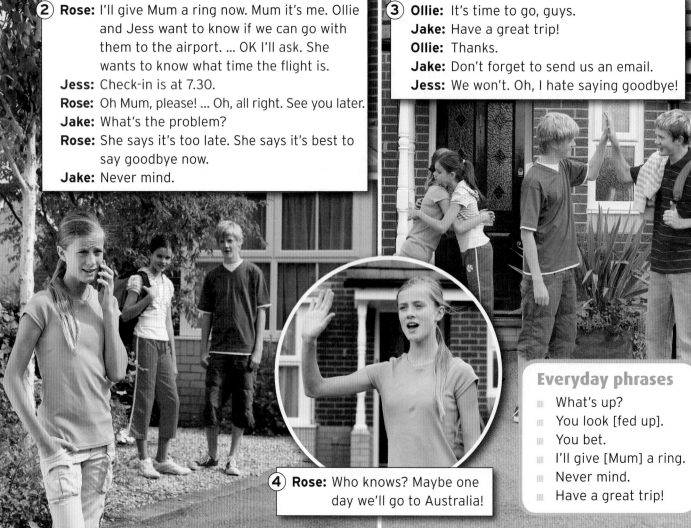

②
Rose: I'll give Mum a ring now. Mum it's me. Ollie and Jess want to know if we can go with them to the airport. ... OK I'll ask. She wants to know what time the flight is.
Jess: Check-in is at 7.30.
Rose: Oh Mum, please! ... Oh, all right. See you later.
Jake: What's the problem?
Rose: She says it's too late. She says it's best to say goodbye now.
Jake: Never mind.

③
Ollie: It's time to go, guys.
Jake: Have a great trip!
Ollie: Thanks.
Jake: Don't forget to send us an email.
Jess: We won't. Oh, I hate saying goodbye!

④ Rose: Who knows? Maybe one day we'll go to Australia!

Everyday phrases
- What's up?
- You look [fed up].
- You bet.
- I'll give [Mum] a ring.
- Never mind.
- Have a great trip!

Look and learn

Reported statements in the present

Direct statement	Reported statement
You can say goodbye now.	She says (that) **we** can say goodbye now.

Reported questions with *if* and *wh-* questions

Direct question	Reported question
Can you go to the airport with **us**?	They want to know if **I/we can** go to the airport with **them**.
What time **is the flight**?	She wants to know what time **the flight is**.

Think about language

In direct questions, the subject comes *before/after* the verb.
In reported questions, the subject comes *before/after* the verb.

2 Check

Read the dialogue and complete the chart.

Who ...		Jess	Rose	Ollie
1	is going to the airport?	✓		✓
2	is fed up?			
3	wants to go with them?			
4	phones her mum?			
5	knows the time of their flight?			
6	gets in the taxi?			

3 Speak

Report what Will is saying on his mobile with *say* or *want to know*.

1   *He says he's finishing his homework.*

1 I'm finishing my homework.

2 It won't take long.

3 I'm leaving at 6.30.

4 I've got a new computer game.

5 What are you doing?

6 Have you done your homework yet?

7 Can you meet me at 7.15?

8 Does the film start at 8 o'clock?

4 🎧 English in action: Saying goodbye

a) Listen. Then practise the conversation.

A: *I'm afraid I must go.*
B: *OK. See you tomorrow.*
A: *Yes, see you.*

A: *It's time to go.*
B: *OK. Have a good holiday.*
A: *Thanks, I will.*
B: *Don't forget to send me a postcard of Florida.*
A: *OK! Bye! Say goodbye to Anna for me.*

A: *I'm going to miss you.*
B: *Me too. Remember to keep in touch.*
A: *I will. Take care! And have a safe journey!*
B: *Thanks. Goodbye!*

b) Act other goodbye scenes.

Goodbye!

How green are you?

1 Which of these do you recycle?
a) newspapers, cans, glass, plastics ☐
b) newspapers and cans ☒ c) newspapers ☐

2 How many times do you use a spray can in a day?
a) 0 ☐ b) 1-4 ☐ c) more than 4 ☐

3 How many kilometres do you and your family travel by car in a day?
a) 0-5 ☐ b) 6-15 ☐ c) more than 15 ☒

4 When you are the last to leave the room, how often do you turn off the light?
a) usually ☒ b) sometimes ☐ c) never ☐

5 How many TVs, stereos and radios do you leave on stand-by?
a) 0 ☐ b) 1-3 ☒ c) more than 3 ☐

6 If you have to make a short journey, do you ...
a) walk or cycle ☒ b) use public transport ☐
c) ask someone to take you by car ☐

7 In winter, what is the average temperature in your home?
a) under 18° ☒ b) 18-20° ☐ c) more than 20° ☐

8 Do you bring shopping home in
a) your own shopping bags ☒ b) re-used plastic bags ☒
c) new plastic bags from the supermarket ☐

How green are <u>you</u>? Look at your score.

Mostly a)s Excellent! You're definitely an eco-warrior.
Mostly b)s You're trying to be green but please try harder!
Mostly c)s You're definitely not green. You must do more to help the environment!

Some facts

- Most scientists say that global warming is caused by carbon dioxide in the earth's atmosphere.
- In 2006, over 26 billion tonnes of carbon dioxide was produced by cars, planes, factories and power stations.
- 10 tonnes of carbon dioxide are produced each year by the average family in Europe
- British shoppers use more than eight billion plastic bags every year.
- Most Irish people have stopped using plastic bags because there is a bag tax.
- It takes only six weeks for a recycled can to be back in the shops.

1 (3/22) Read

Read and do the questionnaire. Find out how green you are.

New words

- recycle · jar · spray can · stand-by
- public transport · packet · wrapped
- shopping bag · reused · eco-warrior
- global warming · carbon dioxide
- atmosphere · factories · power stations

2 Check

Answer the questions.

1 What do scientists think causes global warming?
2 What produces large amounts of carbon dioxide?
3 Why have Irish people stopped using a lot of plastic bags?
4 How long does it take for a can to be recycled?

3 Speak

In groups, think of five things which you and your family can do to help save the environment. Use some of these verbs to help you.

- recycle · reuse · (not) waste · reduce · save
- (not) throw away · (not) buy

1 *We should recycle our cans.*

Study tip

How to listen

- Try to predict what you are going to hear.
- Think about who is speaking and where they are.
- Sometimes there is a text, or some questions or headings in your textbook to help you.
- While you listen, concentrate on the words which carry information. Don't worry about words you don't know.
- If it is possible, listen more than once. First listen for general meaning. Then listen again for detail.

Look at the next listening exercise. What is it about?

4 (3/23) Listen

Listen to two people talking about a famous environmental disaster. Answer the questions.

1 When did the disaster happen?
2 Where did it happen?
3 How much oil was spilt?
4 Which coasts were polluted?
5 How many seabirds were killed?
6 How many years did it take to clean up after the disaster?

Project

Portfolio

A natural or environmental disaster

Write three paragraphs about a natural or an environmental disaster, e.g. a forest fire, a flood, a drought or an oil spill. Use the Internet or the library to find out the details.
Paragraph 1: What happened, when and where?
Paragraph 2: The details of the disaster.
Paragraph 3: The result.

In August 2005, Hurricane Katrina hit the south-east states of the USA. Roads, railways and buildings were destroyed by the storm.

In New Orleans and other towns, thousands of people were trapped by the flood waters. Eventually, people were rescued from their flooded homes. Rescue workers took them to safe places. Sadly, a lot of people were killed or hurt by the hurricane.

After the hurricane, the people started rebuilding their homes. But some people have never gone back.

1 Put the verbs into the present simple passive.

Sailfish Hostel, Daydream Island, Australia

To get to Sailfish Hostel is simple. You ¹ _are taken_ (take) to Daydream Island by boat. There you ²... (meet) by Tommy and Laura and you ³... (show) to your room. All the rooms ⁴... (make) of bamboo and palm leaves.

The Sailfish Hostel isn't five-star. Electricity ⁵... (turn off) at nine in the evening and it ⁶... (not turn on) again till seven in the morning. But you ⁷... (give) torches! You ⁸... (tell) by Tommy and Laura about the danger of sharks and then you ⁹... (leave) on your own to enjoy yourself.

2 🎧 $^3_{24}$ Sounds fun: Elision /d/ + /b/

Listen, then listen and repeat.

Who was it designed by?
It was very cool.
Who was it performed by?
Was it by the school?
Who were they invited by?
Were they friends of yours?
We were quite surprised to see the crowds outside the doors!

3 a) Find the seven materials in this wordsquare.

R	Z	I	A	N	M	R	P	P	D	O	K	W	J	E
C	O	T	T	O	N	E	K	L	R	I	Q	H	O	G
E	R	B	K	L	C	I	T	A	H	T	N	Y	S	R
G	Y	E	N	E	P	Q	B	S	F	S	O	U	G	X
L	Q	N	H	A	R	B	X	T	L	A	R	R	L	A
A	S	C	T	T	U	P	S	I	P	L	U	S	A	V
S	Y	N	T	H	E	T	I	C	F	I	B	R	E	V
S	U	K	M	E	T	A	L	B	T	N	B	F	S	L
R	L	D	Z	R	K	U	L	D	Y	K	E	N	N	S
D	W	U	D	N	D	A	R	O	F	P	R	H	G	A

b) Match the words to the pictures.

leather picture 7

4 a) Rewrite these sentences in the past simple.

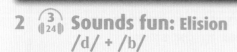

1 The London Eye was opened in 1999.
   They opened the London Eye in 1999.
2 London's first bridge was built by the Romans. _The Romans ..._
3 In the 19ᵗʰ century, more than ten bridges were built across the River Thames. _In the 19ᵗʰ century, they ..._
4 Tower Bridge wasn't designed by Sir Christopher Wren.
   Sir Christopher Wren ...
5 The Houses of Parliament weren't built in the 20ᵗʰ century.
   They ...

b) Rewrite these sentences in the past simple passive.

6 In 1834, fire destroyed the Houses of Parliament.
   In 1834, the Houses of Parliament were destroyed by fire.
7 They started the new Houses of Parliament in 1840.
   The new Houses of Parliament ...
8 They didn't finish the building until 1870. _The building ..._
9 Before 1918, they didn't allow women to vote in Britain.
   Before 1918, women ...
10 Over 400,000 people visited the Houses of Parliament in 2004. _The Houses of Parliament ..._

5 Fill in the missing words.

Last weekend we went for a long walk. To start with we walked down a ¹*hill*, through a ²… , and then round a ³… and over a ⁴… . Then we climbed a ⁵… . At the top we sat down and rested. Then we went down into a ⁶… with a ⁷… at the bottom. We followed the river until we came to the ⁸… . The ⁹… was quite warm so we swam out to a small ¹⁰… . Then we swam back to the beach and had a fantastic picnic.

6 Your parents are speaking to your teacher. They tell you what she says.

1 *She says you are doing well at English.*
2 *She wants to know if …*

1 He's doing well at English.

2 Has he finished his project yet?

3 He's not very good at writing.

4 He mustn't forget his homework.

5 Does he use the Internet for his homework?

6 Has he got any problems?

7 🔊 Chat time

a) Your friend is leaving to go back to the USA. In pairs, follow the cues and write the conversation. Then act it out.

A: *I'm really sorry you're leaving.*
B: *I'm sad too, but I'm afraid it's time to go.*

Student A

Say that you are really sorry that Student B is leaving.

Wish Student B a good journey to the USA.

Say you will. Tell Student B to say goodbye to his/her parents for you.

Student B

Say that you are sad too but you're afraid it's time to go.

Thank Student A. Remind him/her to keep in touch.

Agree. Say goodbye.

b) Listen and compare your conversation.

What can you do?

I can:

- • ask and talk about what things are made of ☐
- • ask and talk about places in the world ☐
- • report what people have said and asked ☐
- • say goodbye ☐

The Night Visitor

1 Our new house is called River Cottage. Well, it's not really new. It's two hundred years old. It used to be a farm worker's cottage. We've got an extra bedroom. Why don't you come and stay with us for a week?

2 Lisa was really pleased when she got the letter from her Aunt Jennie in Devon. The summer holidays were long and a bit boring and she liked her aunt and uncle. When she arrived at the cottage, her aunt took her upstairs. 'I hope you like your room. You're the first person to sleep in it,' her aunt said. Lisa noticed a picture on the wall. 'Who's that lady in the picture?' she asked, 'she looks very sad.'
'I don't know her name,' Aunt Jennie said. 'We found the picture when we were painting the bedroom. She used to live here in River Cottage. Her young husband died in the Great War.' Aunt Jennie continued, 'People say she wore a gold locket with her husband's photo in it every day for the rest of her life. They say she often comes back to the cottage,' Aunt Jennie laughed, 'but I don't believe in ghosts. Let's go and have some supper.'

3 That night Lisa read and then fell asleep. An hour later she woke suddenly. The room was very cold. How strange. It was August! The bedroom door was open. 'That's funny! I'm sure I closed it,' thought Lisa. She was getting out of bed to close the door when she saw a woman in the corner of the room. The woman was looking for something in a cupboard. After a few minutes she disappeared.

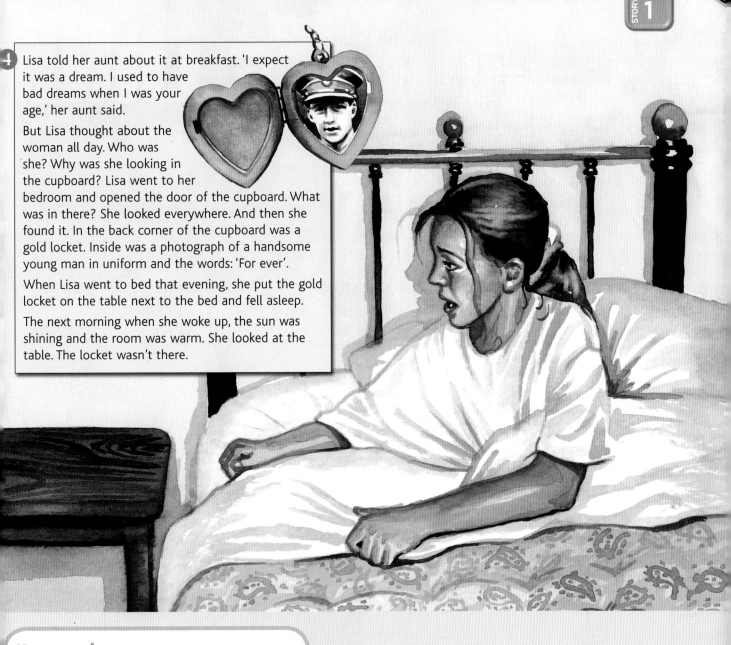

4 Lisa told her aunt about it at breakfast. 'I expect it was a dream. I used to have bad dreams when I was your age,' her aunt said.

But Lisa thought about the woman all day. Who was she? Why was she looking in the cupboard? Lisa went to her bedroom and opened the door of the cupboard. What was in there? She looked everywhere. And then she found it. In the back corner of the cupboard was a gold locket. Inside was a photograph of a handsome young man in uniform and the words: 'For ever'.

When Lisa went to bed that evening, she put the gold locket on the table next to the bed and fell asleep.

The next morning when she woke up, the sun was shining and the room was warm. She looked at the table. The locket wasn't there.

New words

- visitor • farm worker • pleased • sad
- continue • locket • the rest • ghost
- supper • fall asleep • wake • get out of
- disappear • expect • dream

1 🎧 Listen and read

2 Check

Correct the statements.

1 River Cottage is a hundred years old.
   River Cottage is two hundred years old.
2 It used to be an artist's cottage.
3 Lisa's aunt and uncle found the picture of the woman when they were cleaning the house.
4 The woman used to work in River Cottage.
5 Her husband died when he was an old man.
6 The woman always wore a gold ring.

3 Write

Answer the questions.

1 Why did Lisa wake in the middle of the night?
   Because the room was cold.
2 What did she see while she was getting out of bed?
3 What was the woman doing?
4 What did Lisa find at the back of the cupboard?
5 What was in the locket?
6 Where did Lisa put it?
7 What was different when she woke the next morning?

4 Speak

Discuss these questions.

1 Why do you think Lisa's bedroom was cold?
2 What do you think happened to the locket?
3 Do you believe in ghosts?

85

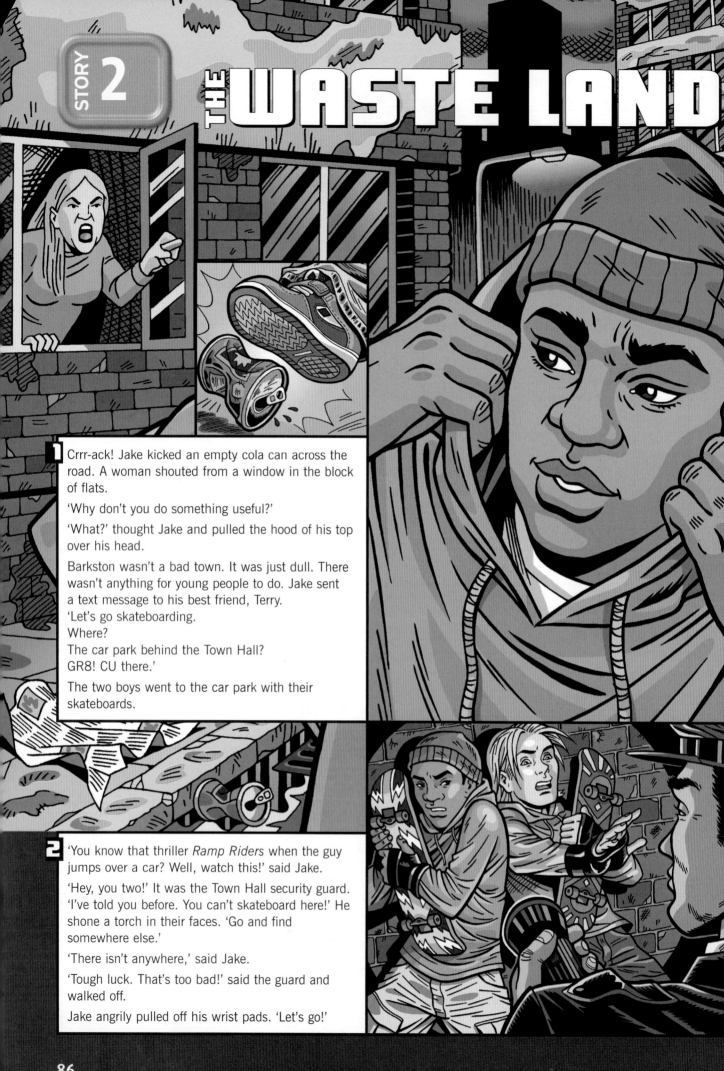

THE WASTE LAND

1 Crrr-ack! Jake kicked an empty cola can across the road. A woman shouted from a window in the block of flats.

'Why don't you do something useful?'

'What?' thought Jake and pulled the hood of his top over his head.

Barkston wasn't a bad town. It was just dull. There wasn't anything for young people to do. Jake sent a text message to his best friend, Terry.
'Let's go skateboarding.
Where?
The car park behind the Town Hall?
GR8! CU there.'

The two boys went to the car park with their skateboards.

2 'You know that thriller *Ramp Riders* when the guy jumps over a car? Well, watch this!' said Jake.

'Hey, you two!' It was the Town Hall security guard. 'I've told you before. You can't skateboard here!' He shone a torch in their faces. 'Go and find somewhere else.'

'There isn't anywhere,' said Jake.

'Tough luck. That's too bad!' said the guard and walked off.

Jake angrily pulled off his wrist pads. 'Let's go!'

3 The two boys put their boards under their arms and walked to the bus stop. As they were getting on the bus, Jake felt in the pocket of his jeans. 'Oh no! I haven't got my bus pass!'

The bus driver was angry, 'Buy a ticket or get off!'

The boys got off the bus and walked along a path under the motorway. The path crossed some waste land where people left rubbish like old fridges, broken bikes and furniture.

'This place has been empty for years. Look at all the rubbish,' said Terry.

Jake stopped. 'Hang on. I've just had an idea. This place is great for a skate park.'

'Dream on!' said Terry. 'What can we do about it?'

Jake paused. 'I'm going to write to the Town Council.' He went home and wrote a letter.

> Dear Members of Barkston Town Council,
> The waste land under the motorway is full of rubbish. It isn't big enough for shops or a sports centre and it's too noisy and dangerous for a children's playground.
> I've got an idea. I think it's perfect for a small skate park.
> Yours sincerely
> Jake Henman (14)

4 Jake posted the letter. Every day he waited for a letter from the council, but nothing came. Eventually he forgot about it.

Six months later, Jake and Terry were going to school across the waste land when they noticed a bulldozer.

'Oh no!' said Jake. He shouted to the man on the bulldozer. 'What are you building?'

'A skate park!' The man started the bulldozer.

Terry smiled at Jake. 'You did it!'

New words

- waste land • kick
- useful • hood • send
- text message • GR8
- guy • security guard
- shine • torch
- tough luck • pull off
- wrist pad • feel
- bus pass • path
- pause • Town Council
- perfect • bulldozer

1 (3/27) **Listen and read**

2 Check

Put the events a)–f) in order to tell the story.

a) He wrote to the council about his idea. ☐

b) One day Jake and Terry were skateboarding in the Town Hall car park. 1

c) They wanted to catch the bus home but Jake didn't have his bus pass. ☐

d) Six months later, the council started to build a skate park on the land. ☐

e) While they were walking home across some waste land, Jake had an idea to build a skate park. ☐

f) A security guard told them to go away. ☐

3 Discuss

What can young people do in your town? What other facilities would you like?

4 Write and act

In groups, write scenes from the story to make a play. Then act it.

Great Expectations
by Charles Dickens

Introduction

About the author

Charles Dickens (1812–1870) is one of England's most famous novelists. His stories take place in Victorian England. He wrote many books, including *David Copperfield* and *Oliver Twist*.

About the story

Pip is an orphan. He lives with his sister, who is married to Joe Gargery, a kind blacksmith, in a village in the south of England. One day Pip helps a convict who has escaped from a prison ship. Pip gives him food.

When he is older, Pip goes to play at the house of a rich woman, Miss Havisham, who has a beautiful adopted daughter called Estella. Miss Havisham is a strange woman. Her fiancé didn't arrive on her wedding day, and since then she has kept her wedding cake and wears only her wedding dress. Pip likes Estella but he thinks she isn't interested in him because he is poor and he has no education. Pip works as a blacksmith in Joe Gargery's forge but he hates the job and wants more from life – and he wants Estella. Then one day a stranger arrives ...

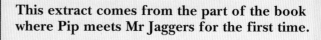

This extract comes from the part of the book where Pip meets Mr Jaggers for the first time.

It was a Saturday night. We were sitting round the fire at the village inn. Then a strange gentleman came up to us and said:

'I believe there may be a blacksmith here called Joe Gargery.'

'That is me,' said Joe.

'You have a young man with you called Pip,' said the stranger. 'Is he here?'

'I am here,' I said.

'I would like to talk to you two in private,' he said.

In silence, we three walked home.

'My name is Jaggers,' he said, 'and I am a lawyer in London. I must tell you that Pip has Great Expectations. Soon he will inherit a lot of money from an anonymous person. This person wants Pip to leave this place and have a gentleman's education in London.'

I could not believe my ears. My dream was coming true.

'I have some money with me for your education and expenses. When will you come to London?'

I said I could come immediately.

'Good. First,' said Mr Jaggers, 'you need some new clothes. I'll leave you twenty pounds. I think it will be good if you leave for London as soon as possible.'

New words

- expectation • novelist • orphan
- blacksmith • convict • escape
- adopted • fiancé • wedding
- forge • stranger • inn • gentleman
- in private • in silence • lawyer
- inherit • anonymous • expenses
- warmly • hug • whistle
- unknown • signpost

1 🎧 3/28 **Listen and read**

2 Check

a) Read the introduction and say if the sentences are true (✓) or false (✗).

1 Charles Dickens wrote about life in England in Victorian times. ✓
2 Joe Gargery is Pip's father.
3 Pip was once kind to an escaped convict.
4 Miss Havisham is Estella's aunt.
5 Miss Havisham is married.
6 Pip likes Estella very much.
7 Pip is a blacksmith.
8 Pip enjoys his life in the village.

b) Read the extract from *Great Expectations* and complete the sentences.

1 When Mr Jaggers first saw Pip and Joe, they were ...
2 The lawyer tells Pip the good news that he will soon ... from ...
3 When Pip left the village, he remembered ... and began to ...

When he left us, Joe locked the front door and we sat by the fire. We didn't speak for a long time. Then Joe got up and held me warmly and said he was pleased for me, but I knew he was very sad.

I left our village at five the next morning. I told Joe that I would prefer to walk away alone. I had a quick breakfast. I kissed my sister and hugged Joe. Then I picked up my bag and left.

I walked fast and whistled. The village was quiet. I remembered my days as a child there. The future was unknown and I began to cry. At the end of the village I put my hand on the village signpost and said, 'Goodbye, my dear, dear friend!'

3 Speak

Talk about these questions.

What do you think happens to Pip next? Who is the anonymous person?

4 🎧 3/29 **Listen**

Listen to a summary of the rest of the story and answer the questions.

1 Who is the anonymous person?
2 Does Pip eventually become rich and happy?
3 Does Pip marry Estella?

The Chrysalids
by John Wyndham

Introduction
About the author

John Wyndham (1903–1969) is a well-known British science-fiction writer of the 20th century. In his books, ordinary people live in an unusual world. His most famous books include *The Day of the Triffids* and *The Midwich Cuckoos*.

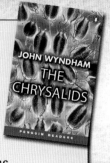

About the story

Some years after a terrible war, some parts of the world are still dead and black. Nothing lives there. In other parts, plants, animals and people grow in strange shapes. David lives in Waknuk. In Waknuk people follow the rules of their group carefully. Their plants and animals must grow correctly. Their children must be perfect. It is wrong to be different. If they are different, they are sent away.

This extract comes from the part of the book where David meets and makes friends with Sophie.

I went out alone that day. I walked along a path through the fields. Then I came to a sandy hill. It was a good place to play. I began to slide down the hill. Then a voice said: 'Hello!'

'Hello,' I answered. A girl stepped out from behind a tree. She had dark hair and she wore a yellow dress.

'What's your name?' I asked her.

'Sophie,' she told me. 'What's yours?'

'David,' I said.

Sophie climbed up the hill and slid down. At the bottom she was laughing.

'Again,' she said.

The third time, she had an accident. She reached the bottom of the hill and did not move. I slid down and stopped next to her.

'What's the matter?' I asked.

'I can't move my foot. It hurts,' she said.

Her left foot was under the sand. I saw that it was caught between two stones.

'We must pull your foot out of your shoe,' I decided.

'No!' she said. 'No, we mustn't.' She was frightened. She began to cry.

I didn't know what to do. I could see that her ankle was twisted. I pulled her foot out of the shoe. The foot was red and hurting. Then I noticed that she had six toes.

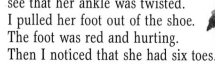

'You must never tell,' she said. 'Never! Promise me?'
I promised.

I took Sophie back home to her mother. When she saw Sophie's foot, she said: 'Nobody must know about Sophie's toes. It is very, very important. People can be very cruel.'

'I promise. Nobody will know,' I said.

In the long summer days Sophie and I often walked in quiet country places. One afternoon we discovered a stream with rocks in it. I took off my shoes and put my feet in the water. Sophie watched me, then she slowly took off her shoes too and stepped into the stream.

Suddenly, a voice called 'Hello, David!'

I looked up. A boy was standing on the side of the stream. I knew him. His name was Alan, he was about two years older than me.

Sophie quickly put on her shoes and walked away.

'Who is she?' asked Alan. 'I've never ...' He suddenly stopped speaking. He was looking hard at the rock next to me. On the rock was a wet footprint. It showed all six toes clearly.

'Oh,' said Alan. 'What's her name?'

I didn't answer. The words of Sophie's mother were in my head. 'Nobody must know. Nobody!' Now this boy did know and it frightened me. If he knew about it, he might tell people. What should I do?

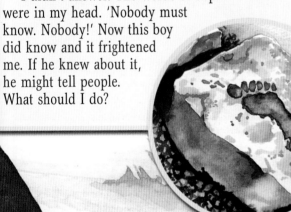

1 Listen and read

2 Check

a) Read the introduction and say if the sentences are true (✓) or false (✗).

1 John Wyndham wrote love stories. ✗
2 There was a terrible war before the story starts.
3 The whole world is dead and black.

b) Read the extract and choose the right ending, a) or b).

1 David first met Sophie when he was
   a) playing on a sandy hill. b) walking home.
2 Sophie hurt her foot when she
   a) slid down the hill. b) took off her shoe.
3 Sophie was different from other children because she a) didn't like wearing shoes.
   b) had six toes on each foot.
4 Alan was a) a friend of David.
   b) someone that David knew from Waknuk.
5 When Alan noticed Sophie's footprint, David
   a) wasn't frightened.
   b) thought that perhaps Sophie was in danger.

3 Speak

Talk about this question.

Think about your country. What is life like for people who are different?

4 Listen

Listen to a summary of the rest of the story and answer the questions.

1 Why is David different?
   He can talk telepathically.
2 Who is Petra?
3 What does David find out about her?
4 What sort of place is *The Fringes*?
5 Where do David and Petra escape to and how?

 # Songs

 Lesson 2, Exercise 7
Dedicated Follower of Fashion: The Kinks

Read the information and listen to the song.

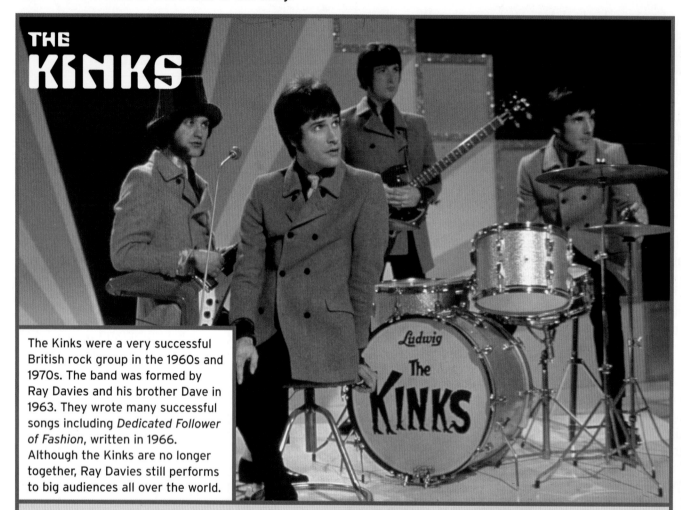

THE KINKS

The Kinks were a very successful British rock group in the 1960s and 1970s. The band was formed by Ray Davies and his brother Dave in 1963. They wrote many successful songs including *Dedicated Follower of Fashion*, written in 1966. Although the Kinks are no longer together, Ray Davies still performs to big audiences all over the world.

Dedicated Follower of Fashion

They seek him here, they seek him there,
His clothes are loud, but never square.
It will make or break him so he's got to buy the best,
'Cause he's a dedicated follower of fashion.

And when he does his little rounds,
Round the boutiques of London Town,
Eagerly pursuing all the latest fads and trends,
'Cause he's a dedicated follower of fashion.

Oh yes, he is (oh yes, he is), oh yes, he is (oh yes, he is).
He thinks he is a flower to be looked at,
This pleasure-seeking individual always looks his best
'Cause he's a dedicated follower of fashion.

Oh yes, he is (oh yes, he is), oh yes, he is (oh yes, he is).
There's one thing that he loves and that is flattery.
One week he's in polka-dots, the next week he is in stripes.
'Cause he's a dedicated follower of fashion.

They seek him here, they seek him there,
In Regent Street and Leicester Square.
Everywhere the Carnabetian army marches on,
Each one a dedicated follower of fashion.

Oh yes, he is (oh yes, he is), oh yes, he is (oh yes, he is).
His world is built 'round discotheques and parties.
This pleasure-seeking individual always looks his best
'Cause he's a dedicated follower of fashion.

Oh yes, he is (oh yes, he is), oh yes, he is (oh yes, he is).
He flits from shop to shop just like a butterfly.
In matters of the cloth he is as fickle as can be,
'Cause he's a dedicated follower of fashion.
He's a dedicated follower of fashion.
He's a dedicated follower of fashion.

The recordings on the CD do not feature the original artists.

Lesson 17, Exercise 8
Have You Ever?: S Club 7

Read the information and listen to the song.

S Club 7 became famous through their TV show in 1998 and released their first single, *Bring It All Back*, in 1999. It went straight to Number One. The band also released their own film (*Seeing Double*) in 2002. The band eventually split up in 2003.

Have You Ever?

Sometimes it's wrong to walk away,
Though you think it's over.
Knowing there's so much more to say,
Suddenly the moment's gone
And all your dreams are upside down
And you just want to change the way
The world goes round.

Chorus
Tell me
Have you ever loved and lost somebody?
Wished there was a chance to say I'm sorry?
Can't you see that's the way I feel about you and
  me, baby?
Have you ever felt your heart was breaking?
Looking down the road you should be taking?
I should know 'cause I loved and lost the day I let you go.

Can't help but think that this is wrong,
We should be together,
Back in your arms where I belong.
Now I finally realize
It was forever that I found,
I'd give it all to change the way
The world goes round.

Chorus

I really want to hear you say
That you know just how it feels,
To have it all and let it slip away.
Can't you see?
I know the moment's gone.
I'm still holding on somehow,
Wishing I could change the way
The world goes round.

Chorus

Lesson 22, Exercise 9
Leaving on a Jet Plane: John Denver

Read the information and listen to the song.

John Denver was one of the world's best-known country and western singers. He was famous as a songwriter, singer and actor. His most popular songs were *Take me home, Country Roads*; *Annie's Song* and *Leaving on a Jet Plane*. John Denver died in a plane crash in California, USA in 1997.

Leaving on a Jet Plane

All my bags are packed,
I'm ready to go.
I'm standing here outside your door,
I hate to wake you up to say goodbye.
But the dawn is breaking,
It's early morn.
The taxi's waiting,
He's blowing his horn.
Already I'm so lonesome I could cry.

Chorus
So kiss me and smile for me.
Tell me that you'll wait for me.
Hold me like you'll never let me go.
I'm leaving on a jet plane,
Don't know when I'll be back again.
Oh babe, I hate to go.

There's so many times I've let you down,
So many times I've played around,
I'll tell you now, they don't mean a thing.
Every place I go, I'll think of you.
Every song I sing, I'll sing for you.
When I come back, I'll wear your wedding ring.

Chorus

Now the time has come to leave you.
One more time let me kiss you
Then close your eyes,
I'll be on my way.
Dream about the days to come,
When I won't have to leave alone,
About the time, I won't have to say.

Chorus

Leaving on a jet plane,
Don't know when I'll be back again.
Oh babe, I hate to go.

Lesson 33, Exercise 8

Sweet Dreams My L.A. Ex: Rachel Stevens

Read the information and listen to the song.

Rachel Stevens started her music career with S-Club-7 in 1998. After having four Number Ones, she left the band for a solo career. *Sweet Dreams My L.A. Ex* was her first single, it was released in 2003 and was a hit. Her second single, *Some Girls*, reached Number One in 2004.

Sweet Dreams My L.A. Ex

Hey, hang your red gloves up
'Cause there's nothing left to prove now.
Hey, hang your red gloves up
Baby, no one cares but you.
What planet are you from?
Accuse me of things that I never done,
Listen to you carrying on,
Cheating another love song.

Chorus
If I were in your shoes,
I'd whisper before I shout.
Can't you stop playing that record again?
Find somebody else to talk about.
If I were in your shoes,
I'd worry of the effects.
You've had your say but now it's my turn,
Sweet dreams my L.A. Ex.

We've had it on full steam,
'Til the light comes back to you now.
Hey, is it all it seems?
Is it all you dreamed and more?
What planet are you from?
Accuse me of things that I never done,
Listen to you carrying on,
Cheating another love song.

Chorus

Does it make you feel the man
Pointing the finger because you can?
I spell it loud and clear,
Baby, that tongue's not welcome around here.

You turned the city round (L.A. Ex).
Do you think I give a damn (L.A. Ex)?
Do you think that I'm fairer (L.A. Ex)?
Sweet dreams my L.A. Ex.

Chorus

Limericks

Lesson 3, Exercise 9

Listen and complete.

A hungry young schoolboy called Pete
Was desperate for something to ¹... .
So he bought a ²... ,
But fell over a log
And ³... the ⁴... in the ⁵... !

Lesson 7, Exercise 8

Listen and complete.

A silly young man from Peru
Once dreamt he ¹... his shoe.
He awoke in the ²...
With a terrible fright
And ³... that his nightmare was ⁴... .

Lesson 23, Exercise 9

Listen and complete.

There was a young girl called Colette
Who started a job as a ¹... .
Her first task – can you ²...?
Was a duck in distress,
But she ³... in the pond and got ⁴... !

Lesson 27, Exercise 9

Listen and complete.

In a ¹... a man called Carew,
Once found a ²... fly in his stew
Said the waiter, 'Don't ³... !
If you wave it about,
The others will all ⁴... one too!'

Welcome to Max's Grammar Store! Open the doors and choose!

Max's Grammar Store

1 Present simple tense
2 Present continuous tense
3 Object pronoun: *one(s)*
4 *Going to* future for plans and intentions
5 Present continuous for future arrangements
6 Past simple tense
7 Modal: *could/couldn't* (ability)
8 Past continuous tense
9 Conjunctions: *when* and *while*
10 Modal: *used to*
11 Determiners: *too* and *enough*
12 Defining relative clauses with *who*, *which* and *where*
13 Pronouns: *someone/something/somewhere*; *anyone/anything/anywhere*; *no one/nothing/nowhere*
14 Present perfect simple tense with *just*, *already* and *yet*, with *ever/never* and with *for* and *since*
15 Future simple: *will/won't* (predictions) *Will/won't* (offers, promises and decisions)
16 Modal: *would*, *would rather* and *would prefer to*
17 Zero conditional
18 First conditional (+ *will*) Future time clause (+ *when*)
19 Modal: *may*
20 Modals: *must/mustn't/have to* (obligation and prohibition)
21 Modal: *should/shouldn't* (advice)
22 Second conditional (+ *would*) (+ *might*)
23 Present simple passive
24 Past simple passive
25 Reported statements and questions in the present
26 Irregular past tense verbs

1 Present simple tense

Positive

I live in Melbourne.
You like films.
He comes from Sydney.
She likes volleyball.
It eats meat.
We go to school.
You play a lot of sport.
They want to be famous.

Negative

I don't live in London.
You don't like pizza.
He doesn't come from Manchester.
She doesn't like football.
It doesn't eat plants.
We don't work in a shop.
You don't play computer games.
They don't want to go to school.

***Yes/No* questions**

Do you live in London?
Yes, I do./No, I don't.
Does your sister go to this school?
Yes, she does./No, she doesn't.

2 Present continuous tense

Positive

I'm waiting for my friend.
You're doing your homework.
He's signing an autograph.
She's eating some chips.
It's running.
We're having a cup of coffee.
You're writing an email.
They're changing some money.

Negative

I'm not waiting for a bus.
You aren't watching TV.
He isn't reading a book.
She isn't buying a CD.
It isn't walking.
We aren't having a meal.
You aren't writing a letter.
They aren't signing autographs.

***Yes/No* questions**

Are you doing your homework?
Yes, I am./No, I'm not.
Is he playing tennis?
Yes, he is./No, he isn't.

3 Object pronoun: *one(s)*

£19.99
£22.50

Which **one** do you like?
I like the red **one**.

£8
£7

Which **ones** do you want?
I want the black **ones**.

(4) *Going to* future for plans and intentions

Positive	Negative	Yes/No questions
I'm going to buy some chips.	I'm not going to have an English lesson.	Are you going to buy a CD?
You're going to do your homework.	You aren't going to play football.	Yes, I am./No, I'm not.
He's going to meet his friend today.	He isn't going to read a book.	Is she going to meet him later?
She's going to invite him to her party.	She isn't going to listen to music.	Yes, she is./No, she isn't.
We're going to play tennis.	We aren't going to buy a tracksuit.	
You're going to watch TV.	You aren't going to eat a pizza.	
They're going to see a film.	They aren't going to use the computer.	

(5) Present continuous for future arrangements

Positive	Negative	Yes/No questions
I'm meeting my friend today.	I'm not meeting my brother.	Are we leaving at six o'clock?
You are going to the doctor tomorrow.	You aren't going to the dentist.	Yes, we are./No, we aren't.
He's eating at a pizza restaurant tonight.	He isn't eating at a Chinese restaurant.	
She's visiting her aunt next week.	She isn't visiting her grandparents.	
We're watching *Shrek 3* on Sunday.	We aren't watching *Spider-Man 3*.	
They're playing Arsenal on Saturday.	They aren't playing Manchester United.	

(6) Past simple tense

Positive	Negative	Yes/No questions
I started school yesterday.	I didn't play volleyball yesterday.	Did you arrive last Tuesday?
You arrived a few days ago.	You didn't start tennis lessons today.	Yes, I did./No, I didn't.
He played rugby last week.	He didn't watch TV.	Did they start piano lessons a week ago?
She invited me to her party.	She didn't live in London a year ago.	Yes, they did./No, they didn't.
It rained a few hours ago.	It didn't happen.	
We decided to go on holiday.	We didn't save any money.	
You finished your homework.	You didn't score a goal.	
They returned home a week ago.	They didn't invite me to the party last week.	

(7) Modal: *could/couldn't* (ability)

Positive	Negative	Yes/No questions
I could swim.	I couldn't draw well.	Could you ride a bike when you were four?
You could speak.	You couldn't do your homework.	Yes, I could./No, I couldn't.
He could draw.	He couldn't believe it.	Could he do up his shoes when he was five?
She could spell.	She couldn't communicate.	Yes, he could./No, he couldn't.
It could run.	It couldn't walk.	
We could tell a story.	We couldn't understand.	
You could speak Italian.	You couldn't speak English.	
They could play tennis.	They couldn't read.	

8 Past continuous tense

Positive

I was sleeping.
You were playing tennis.
He was washing his car.
She was having dinner.
It was flying.
We were playing cards.
You were eating.
They were watching TV.

Negative

I wasn't walking.
You weren't listening.
He wasn't playing the guitar.
She wasn't doing her homework.
It wasn't eating.
We weren't working.
You weren't swimming.
They weren't cooking.

Yes/No questions

Was it snowing?
Yes, it was./No, it wasn't.

Were you doing your homework
 at 7 o'clock last night?
Yes, I was./No, I wasn't.

9 Conjunctions: *when* and *while*

I was doing my homework **when** the telephone rang.
While I was doing my homework, the telephone rang.

They were driving home **when** they saw an accident.
While they were driving home, they saw an accident.

10 Modal: *used to*

Positive

I used to play the drums.
You used to have long wavy hair.
He used to live in Australia.
She used to work in an office.
It used to bite.
We used to like soaps.
You used to eat meat.
They used to watch a lot of TV.

Negative

I didn't use to play the guitar.
You didn't use to have short hair.
He didn't use to live in the USA.
She didn't use to be famous.
It didn't use to drink water.
We didn't use to like sitcoms.
You didn't use to be vegetarian.
They didn't use to do their homework.

Yes/No questions

Did you use to live in Italy?
Yes, I did./No, I didn't.

Did she use to be a singer?
Yes, she did./No, she didn't.

11 Determiners: *too* and *enough*

This skirt is **too** casual.
This skirt is not smart **enough**.

These trousers are **too** short.
These trousers are not long **enough**.

12 Defining relative clauses with *who*, *which* and *where*

I like people **who** are friendly.
It is a film **which** has a lot of action in it.
This is the school **where** they met.

13 Pronouns: *someone/something/somewhere; anyone/anything/anywhere; no one/nothing/nowhere*

Someone made a cake.
I saw **something** on the floor.
The football was **somewhere**
 in the garden.

There wasn't **anyone** at the door.
It isn't **anything** important.
We couldn't find him **anywhere**.

No one came to the party.
There was **nothing** interesting on TV.
I have **nowhere** to put my stuff.

(14) Present perfect simple tense with *just, already* and *yet*

Positive

I've **just** scored a goal.
She's **already** seen the film.
We've **just** done our exercises.
They've **already** done their homework.

Negative

England haven't scored **yet**.
She hasn't seen the film **yet**.
We haven't been for a run **yet**.
They haven't had dinner **yet**.

Yes/No questions

Have you found the ball **yet**?
Yes, I have./No, I haven't.
Has she scored a goal **yet**?
Yes, she has./No, she hasn't.
Have they won the tournament **yet**?
Yes, they have./No, they haven't.

with *ever* and *never*

Have you **ever** been to the USA?
Yes, I have. I went there two years ago.
No, I haven't. I've **never** been there.

Have you **ever** seen the London Eye?
Yes, I have. I saw it last summer.
No, I haven't. I've **never** seen it.

with *for* and *since*

Positive

I've lived in England **since** I was five.
I've lived in England **for** eight years.

Negative

I haven't been to the cinema **since** January.
I haven't been to the cinema **for** three months.

Question

How long have you been here?
For two hours./**Since** one o'clock.

(15) Future simple: *will ('ll)* and *will not (won't)* for predictions

Positive

People **will** wear computers on their wrists.

Negative

People **won't** wear computers on their wrists.

Yes/No question

Will cars use petrol?
Yes, they **will**./No, they **won't**.

Will/won't for offers, promises and decisions

I**'ll** buy the food.
We**'ll** make the sandwiches.
I **won't** be long.

Remember to blow up the balloons.
Yes, I **will**.
Don't forget to borrow some CDs.
No, we **won't**.

(16) Modal: *would/wouldn't*

Positive

I**'d** (**would**) like to be a vet.

Negative

I **wouldn't** like to be a hairdresser.

Yes/No question

Would you like to be a football manager?
Yes, I **would**./No, I **wouldn't**.

would rather and would prefer to

Which **would** you **rather** be, a computer engineer or an electrician?
I**'d rather** be a computer engineer.

Which **would** you **prefer** to be, a web designer or a pilot?
I**'d prefer** to be a web designer.

(17) Zero conditional

If I'm late home from school, my mum **gets** very angry.
If I'm on my mobile, my brother **turns up** the TV.

Question

Does your mum **get** angry if you **don't do** your homework?

18 First conditional (+ will)

I'll be home at three o'clock **if you want** to speak to me.

If you don't get a good mark in your test, your dad **will be** angry.

Question

Will the ice cream melt if I don't put it in the freezer?

Future time clause (+ when)

I'll turn off the television **when he arrives**.
We**'ll have** a drink **when we get** to the café.

Question

Will you call me **when you get** there?

19 Modal: may

I **may** see my friends later.
It **may** snow in December.
We **may** miss the bus. Hurry up!

20 Modals: must/mustn't/have to (obligation and prohibition)

must

I **must** do my homework today.
You **mustn't** walk on the grass.

have to

I **have to** get up early for school.
I **don't have to** get up early at the weekend.

21 Modal: should/shouldn't (advice)

You **should** take some cough medicine.
You **shouldn't** go to school for a few days.

22 Second conditional

(+ would)

If I **won** some money, **I'd (would)** spend it on clothes.
If I **won** some money, I **wouldn't** save it.

Question

If you **won** some money, what **would** you buy?

(+ might)

If I **won** some money, I **might** buy a mobile phone or I **might** travel to the USA.

23 Present simple passive

Positive

The hotel is built of ice.
The sleeping bags are made of synthetic fibre.

Negative

The hotel isn't built of wood.
The beds aren't made of ice.

Yes/No questions

Is the bag made of plastic?
Yes, it is./No, it isn't.

Were the photos taken by your friends?
Yes, they were./No, they weren't.

24 Past simple passive

Positive

Gunpowder was used to blow up some buildings.
Over two square kilometres of the city were destroyed.

Negative

This bag wasn't made in Italy.
Houses south of the river weren't damaged by the fire.

Yes/No questions

Was the fire put out by the baker?
Yes, it was./No, it wasn't.

Were the watches made in the UK?
Yes, they were./No, they weren't.

25 Reported statements and questions in the present

Direct statement

You have to do your homework.
Mum says (that) **I** have to do my homework.

Reported statement

You can go to the party.
Dad says (that) **we** can go to the party.

Direct question

Can **you** send me a postcard?
He wants to know **if I/we** can send him a postcard.

Reported question

When do **you** want to meet?
She wants to know when **we** want to meet.

(26) Irregular past tense verbs

Infinitive	Past	Past participle
be	was/were	been
beat	beat	beaten
become	became	become
begin	began	begun
blow	blew	blown
break	broke	broken
breed	bred	bred
build	built	built
burn	burnt	burnt
burst	burst	burst
buy	bought	bought
catch	caught	caught
choose	chose	chosen
come	came	come
do	did	done
draw	drew	drawn
drive	drove	driven
fall	fell	fallen
feel	felt	felt
fight	fought	fought
find	found	found
fly	flew	flown
get	got	got
give	gave	given
go	went	gone
have	had	had
hear	heard	heard
hit	hit	hit
hurt	hurt	hurt
keep	kept	kept

Infinitive	Past	Past participle
know	knew	known
lean	leant	leant
learn	learnt	learnt
leave	left	left
lose	lost	lost
make	made	made
meet	met	met
put	put	put
read	read	read
ride	rode	ridden
run	ran	run
say	said	said
see	saw	seen
sell	sold	sold
send	sent	sent
shine	shone	shone
sit	sat	sat
slide	slid	slid
spend	spent	spent
spill	spilt	spilt
steal	stole	stolen
take	took	taken
teach	taught	taught
tell	told	told
think	thought	thought
throw	threw	thrown
wake	woke	woken
wear	wore	worn
win	won	won
write	wrote	written

Bye! Keep in touch!

Word list

Lesson 1
Places in town

accent
airline company
Australian
autograph
City Airport
Cool!
Excuse me!
future
Great!
Hollywood
Melbourne
moment
Oh, right.
Quick!
right now
spy
What's
  happening?

Lesson 2
Money

All right.
change (n)
cycle helmet
Don't be late.
Don't be silly.
Hang on!
Here you are.
How much [is
  this helmet]?
Hurry up [you
  two].
See you!
stripe
sunglasses
Sure.

Lesson 3
*Free time
  activities*

cash machine
crazy
do the right
  thing
games shop
Guess what
  [happened].
honest
I nearly forgot.
It was fun/
  rubbish.
lucky
mistake
Please write
  back soon.

rubbish
shopping centre
signed photo
Thanks very
  much for the
  [CD].
wash (v)
Xbox

Lesson 4

apartment
bell
bend
Canary Wharf
clock
corridor
destination
diameter
docks
eastern
Greenwich
hemisphere
Houses of
  Parliament
instead
kilometre
marathon
mark (v)
offices
palace
prisoner
River Thames
side
tower
trip (n)
tunnel
western

Lesson 5

dirty
dishwasher
Swedish

Lesson 6
Verbs of action

completely
escape
film director
finally
happiest
hunters
leaves
nobody
simple
southern
take back
twice
understand
wild

Lesson 7
*Prepositions of
  motion*

across
along
around
into
out of
over
past
through
under

alarm
campers
campsite
celebrate
direction
dramatic
drop (v)
early
eventually
field
firefighter
forest fire
fortunately
helicopter
hotter
plane
really
sand
smoke

Lesson 8
*Musical
  instruments*

accordion
acoustic guitar
drums
electric guitar
flute
harmonica
keyboards
piano
recorder
saxophone
trombone
trumpet
violin

[Jess] must
  you?
[Ollie,] don't be
  so mean [to
  your sister].
... not any more.
Come on,
  [Rose].
designer
  clothes

earn
Here goes.
[I'm] hopeless.
I'm not bad.
karaoke
mike
Not really.
orchestra
ordinary
professional
sports car
TV reporter
You sound like
  [a sick goat].

Lesson 9

ancient
astronomer
believe
calculated
centre
change (v)
circumference
dome
entire
everyone
exactly
flat
fool
grave
idea
Law
mathematician
Medicine
moved
movement
published
skull
solar system
telescope
thousands
turn (v)
universe
upside down
watched

Lesson 10

bad at
gate
good at
pond
runner
swimmer
teenager

Lesson 11
Clothes

anorak
belt
cardigan

coat
mini skirt
sandals
shorts
sweater
tracksuit
vest

Patterns

checked
flowery
patterned
plain
spotted
striped

Styles

baggy
casual
long
loose
short
smart
tight

Can I try this
  [pink anorak]
  on?
choose
fancy dress
  party
It's a bit
  [flowery].
leather
modern
size
What about
  [this spotted
  skirt]?
What do you
  think of [this
  dress]?
You're so [old-
  fashioned]!

Lesson 12
Film types

action film
cartoon/
  animated film
comedy
fantasy film
historical film
horror film
musical
science fiction
  film
western

camp (n)
criminal

deadly
enemy agent
entertaining
excellent
fight
king
ogre
performance
princess
schoolboy
secret service
  agency
suitable
super
task
virus

Lesson 13
*Shapes and
  textures*

bendy
dull
hard
rough
round
shiny
smooth
soft
square
straight
thick
thin

agree
canal
edge
fishing
lost
mystery
sculpture
thieves
threw
tortoise
valuable
well-known

Lesson 14

Cantonese
community
cultures
curry
education
ethnic
European
European Union
freedom
minority
mixture
multicultural
New Year

nowadays
occasions
Pakistani
population
races
satellite
special occasion
tradition
Urdu
well-paid

Lesson 15
Ireland

Lesson 16
Words to do
  with sports
beat (*v*)
draw (*n*)
draw (*v*)
lose
match (*n*)
pass (*v*)
play (*v*)
score (*n*)
score (*v*)
stop
tackle (*v*)
team
tournament
whistle
win (*v*)

Come on [Joe]!
Dream on!
goal
Hi guys!
hot dog
Put the ball in
  the net!
scored
That's good.
There's still a
  chance.
We're useless!
You always say
  that!

Lesson 17
Travel
double-decker
  bus
scooter
plane
mountain bike
taxi
motorbike
long distance
  coach
caravan
lorry
helicopter
high-speed train

all night
anywhere
questionnaire

rides
somewhere

Lesson 18
Types of book
adventure story
biography
detective story
fairy tale
fantasy book
ghost story
historical novel
romantic novel
science fiction
  book
short story

[I haven't seen
  it] for ages.
badly
better
book club
borrowed
character
chosen
Come and sit
  down.
Don't
  exaggerate!
horse whisperer
It's brilliant.
Sorry I'm late.
starving
That's OK.
truck

Lesson 19
aborigines
advice
Ayers Rock
bumpy
camel
Channel Tunnel
continent
crazy
desert
driest
Eiffel Tower
Eurostar
farming
flattest
lowest
miss
motorcyclist
narrow
overseas
Paris
Perth
race (*v*)
railway line
Sydney
track
transport

Lesson 20
foreign

Lesson 21
Technology
connect to the
  Internet
disc
download music
download
  software
keyboard
laptop
memory
microchip
modem
monitor
mouse
PC (personal
  computer)
screen
search the web
send/receive an
  email
send/receive a
  text message
software
surf the
  Internet
website

average
brain
cheerful
communicate
control
cooker
disabled
object
phone box
post box
predict
several
tiny

Lesson 22
Furniture and
  furnishings
blind(s)
chest of
  drawers
curtains
cushion
lamp
mirror
radiator
rug
tablecloth
wardrobe
waste bin

Don't worry.
Fine.
Good idea.
How's it going?
I bet [it's Ranu].
I'll give you a
  hand.
Mind [that paint
  pot].
paint (*v*)

paintbrush
There's
  someone at
  the door.

Lesson 23
Jobs
carpenter
computer
  engineer
detective
doctor
electrician
firefighter
footballer
football
  manager
hairdresser
journalist
model
pilot
plumber
police officer
racing-car
  driver
ski instructor
sports reporter
TV newsreader
TV reporter
vet
web designer

ambition
crash (*n*)
I think it sounds
  interesting.
I'm not sure.
motorway
No wonder!
politician
programme
  seller
stadium
That's no
  surprise.
Typical!
You're [football
  crazy].
You're so
  [bossy].

Lesson 24
a couple of
adverts
cable
channel
characters
concentrate
good-looking
non-stop
reality TV
satellite
TV set
vote
wars
widescreen
wildlife

Lesson 25
crowded
oil

Lesson 26
Personality
  adjectives (1)

Personality
  adjectives (2)
annoying
bad-tempered
big-headed
dishonest
easy-going
generous
greedy
honest
impatient
loyal
mean
modest
moody
patient
sensible
tidy
untidy

... not fair
[Until] at least
  [nine o'clock].
[You're] in a
  bad mood
  [today]!
... all the time.
attention
bedtime
He gets on my
  nerves.
maybe
normal
occasionally
On the whole
  [he sounds
  fairly normal]!
perhaps
probably
problem
spend time with
strict
tell the truth
volume
younger

Lesson 27
Food and drink

Cooking verbs
bake
beat
boil
burn
chop
cook
fry
heat
melt
mix

peel
pour
serve
slice
sprinkle
taste

frying pan
gently
grated
grill (*n*)
mixed herbs
olive oil
oven
pepper
pizza base
ready-made
recipe
saucepan
tap

Lesson 28
Phrasal verbs
get on/get off
pick up/put
  down
put on/take off
throw away
turn on/turn off
wake up

Be careful!
bite
flash (*n*)
Get ready!
Gosh, [it's hot]!
huge
I'm baking.
Is it all right
  if I [take a
  photo]?
just in time
mummy
No, not yet.
pyramids
shark
sting ray
There's one!

Lesson 29
blog
crash (*v*)
essays
font
homework
image
insert images
instant
  messaging
keep in touch
log onto
online
penfriend
picture
preview
print
ring tones

share
  experiences
Skype
style
text
toolbar
up-to-date
Webcam

Lesson 30
in a bad mood
recharging

Lesson 31
Sports places
course
court
park
pitch
pool
ring
rink
track

... that's all.
athletics
boxing
equipment
hole
ice skating
In fact [I've
  never done it
  in one stroke].
It's my turn
  now.
mini-golf
players
rules
stroke (n)
term time
That's cheating!
That's not bad.
What a [brilliant
  stroke]!

Lesson 32
Common
  illnesses
a cold
a cough
a headache
a sore throat
a stomachache
a temperature

[Rose's] right.
aspirin
blister
fun run
heel
I'm a bit
  [worried].
ill
Just to be sure.
medicine
tablets
Well done!

What's the
  matter [with
  you]?

Lesson 33
Adjectives with
  prepositions
bored with
fond of
good at
interested in
keen on
mad about
proud of
scared of

bedclothes
chase
faint
situation
skating
vase

Lesson 34
adult prison
army
babysitter
bank account
blood
definitely
delivered
election
fed up
full-time
helmet
legal
moped
own
part-time
tattoo

Lesson 35
awake
Biology
Chemistry
flu
moo (v)
racket
spider
toast

Lesson 36
Materials
cotton
glass
leather
metal
paper
plastic
rubber
synthetic fibre
wood
wool

beginning
carved
degrees
electricity
foam rubber

heated
ice
mattress
moon boots
provided
sculptor
sleeping bag
Sweden
woolly
zero

Lesson 37
Buildings and
  landscape
church
cathedral
monument
mountain
ocean
sea
river
forest
desert
lake
coast
valley
hill
stream
island

architect
area
baker
balcony
blow up
burned
burnt down
certificate
close together
column
commemorate
created
destroyed
earthquake
experiment
fire
firebreaks
flames
gravity
gunpowder
homeless
laboratory
luckily
managed
miles
morning
officially
ruined
San Francisco
sparks
spreading
stopped

Lesson 38
ask
check-in
have a safe
  journey

Have a great
  trip!
I'll give [Mum] a
  ring.
Never mind.
What's up?
You bet.
You look [fed
  up].

Lesson 39
atmosphere
bottle
carbon dioxide
clean up
disaster
drought
eco-warrior
factories
global warming
jar
natural
oil spill
packet
power stations
public transport
recycle
reduce
reused
seabird
shopping bag
spray can
stand-by
tax
wrapped

Lesson 40
bamboo
enjoy
palm leaves

Story 1
continue
disappear
dream
expect
fall asleep
farm worker
get out of
ghost
locket
pleased
the rest
sad
supper
visitor
wake

Story 2
bulldozer
bus pass
facilities
feel
GR8
guy
hood
kick
path

pause
perfect
pull off
security guard
send
shine
text message
torch
tough luck
Town Council
useful
waste land
wrist pad

Story 3
adopted
anonymous
blacksmith
convict
escape
expectation
expenses
fiancé
forge
gentleman
hug (v)
inherit
inn
in private
in silence
lawyer
novelist
orphan
signpost
stranger
unknown
warmly

Story 4
ankle
bottom
catch
correctly
cruel
deviation
different
footprint
frightened
hurt
laugh
notice
ordinary
sandy
side
slide
step out
telepathic
toe
twisted
unusual
voice
war

Pearson Education Limited,
Edinburgh Gate, Harlow
Essex, CM20 2JE, England
and Associated Companies throughout the world

www.pearsonelt.com

© Brian Abbs, Ingrid Freebairn and Pearson Education Limited 2009

First published 2009
Fourth impression 2014
Set in 10.5/14pt Interstate Light
Printed in China (GCC/04)
ISBN 978-1-4058-7479-3

Designed by Roarrdesign
Location photography by Gareth Boden
Art direction by Hilary Fletcher
Picture research by Kath Kolberg

Illustrated by: Tim Archbold (Graham-Cameron Illustration) pages 12 bottom left and bottom right; 22 middle right; 25 right; 28; 35; 52 top right; 55 top right; 59 top left; 62 top right, 94; 98 top left; Kathryn Baker (Sylvie Poggio) pages 84/85; 90/91; David Banks pages 12 top left; 17 right; 22 top left; 29 bottom right; 32 bottom left; 61 bottom left; Humberto Blanco (Sylvie Poggio) pages 12 top right; 44; 45 right; 68; Peter Dennis (Linda Rogers Associates) page 72 bottom left; Roger Fereday (Linda Rogers Associates) page 82 top left; Brett Hudson (Graham-Cameron Illustration) pages 32 top left and middle left; 62 top left and right; Joanna Kerr pages 14 bottom left; 22 bottom right; 23 bottom left; 32 top right; 42 top left; 43 bottom left; 47; 52 bottom left; 55 bottom left; 56; 63 right; 67 right; 69; 72 top left and top right; 75; 83 bottom; Brian Leith (Bright Agency) pages 88/98; Sean Longcroft pages 7 bottom left; 18; 23 middle left; 26; 32 middle right; 36; 43 bottom right; 45 top left; 62 bottom left; 63 bottom left; 73 left and right; 75; 82; 95; Frano Petrusa (Beehive Illustration) for characterisation of Max throughout; Wes Lowe (Beehive Illustration) pages 20; 23 top left; 33 top left; 69 top right; 82 top left; David Shenton pages 22 top right; 33 middle right; 42 bottom right; 52 left; 71; 72 bottom left; Martin Shovel pages 16 top; 17 top left; 27; 59 bottom right; 66; 67 left; 72 middle right; Jane Smith page 40 top; Theresa Tibbetts (Beehive Illustration) page 25 left; Richard Williams (Eastwing) pages 86/87.

Authors' acknowledgements

We would like to thank the many teachers and advisors in Italy, Poland, Spain and Portugal for their very useful comments and suggestions during the rewriting of this course.

Brian Abbs and Ingrid Freebairn

Acknowledgements

We are grateful to the following for permission to reproduce copyright material:

Faber Music Limited and Music Sales Limited for the lyric reproduction of *Sweet Dreams my L.A. Ex* words and music by Cathy Dennis, Pontus Winnberg, Christian Karisson and Henrik Jonback copyright © 2003 Murlyn Songs AB and Universal Music Publishing Limited. EMI Music Publishing, London WC2H 0QY. Reproduced by permission of International Music Publications (a trading name of Faber Music Ltd) and Music Sales Limited. All Rights Reserved. International Copyright Secured; Faber Music Limited and Warner/Chappell Music Ltd for the lyric reproduction of *Have You Ever?* words and music by Andrew Frampton, Cathy Dennis and Christopher Braide copyright © 2001 EMI Music Publishing Ltd, Visible Music Ltd. & EMI Music Publishing Ltd, London WC2H 0QY. Reproduced by permission of International Music Publications (a trading name of Faber Music Ltd) and Visible Music Ltd administered by Warner/Chappell Music Ltd, London W6 8BS. All Rights Reserved. Reproduced by permission; Carlin Music Corporation for the lyric reproduction of *Dedicated Follower of Fashion* by Ray Davies copyright © 1966 Davray Music Ltd and Carlin Music Corp. London NW1 8BD. All Rights Reserved. Used by permission; Harmony Music Ltd for the lyric reproduction of *Leaving on a Jet Plane* words and music by John Denver copyright © Harmony Music Ltd. Administered by Bucks Music Group Limited. Used by permission; Pearson Education Limited for an extract from the simplified edition of *Great Expectations* by Charles Dickens; David Higham Associates Limited for an extract from *The Chrysalids* by John Wyndham.

The publisher would like to thank the following for their kind permission to reproduce their photographs:
(Key: b-bottom; c-centre; l-left; r-right; t-top)

A1 Pix: 81; Alamy Images: Adrian Buck 70t; Arco Images 29, 41l; Bill Bachmann 15b; Cephas Picture Library 40; David Ball 82b; David Levenson 10/1; David R. Frazier Photolibrary, Inc. 49b; Hideo Kurihara 10/2, 41r; Imagebroker 70cl; Janine Wiedel Photolibrary 51t; Jason Lindsey 74b; Jeff Smith 80b; Kolvenbach 74t; Mary Evans Picture Library 21l; Patrick Ward 10/5; © Pearson Education, taken on commission by Gareth Boden: 4, 5tr, 6, 8b, 8t, 9, 15t, 18, 24, 34, 35b, 35t, 36, 38, 46, 48, 54, 57, 58, 62, 64, 66, 75, 78; Popperfoto 65b; The Print Collector 20c; Robert Harding Picture Library Ltd 77; Sergio Pitamitz 10/6; Shout 70b; SuperStock 60tc; Alton Towers: 37; BBC Photo Library: 53; Corbis: 16, 28br, 93r; Albrecht G. Schaefer 40t; Comstock Select 30t; Jose Luis Pelaez Inc/Blend Images 70cr; Kevin Dodge 60bc; Martin Harvey 40b; Sergio Pitamitz/Zefa 10/3; Tim Tadder 54t; Tony Marsh/ Reuters 5b; Getty Images: 41c, 76b, 80cl, 80t; Ana Ce 80cr; Asia Images 30b, 60t; Hulton Archive 76t, 92; National Geographic 40c; Roger Viollet 14; Taxi 10/4 (5), 65t; Ronald Grant Archive: 27; Kobal Collection Ltd: 26; Moviestore Collection Ltd: 39; Photofusion Picture Library: 31; PunchStock: Upper cut 60b; Rail Images: 41; Retna Pictures Ltd 93l, 94; Rex Features: Chris Harris 18l; Ken McKay 24b; Science Photo Library Ltd: Detlev Van Ravensway 20t

Every effort has been made to trace the copyright holders and we apologise in advance for any unintentional omissions. We would be pleased to insert the appropriate acknowledgement in any subsequent edition of this publication.

Special thanks to the following for their help during location photography:

Arsenal Football Club www.arsenal.com; Associated Taxis, Bishop's Stortford; Bishop's Stortford College; Café Rouge, Hertford www.caferouge.co.uk; Halfords, Harlow www.halfords.com; The London Aquarium, www.londonaquarium.co.uk; The Murtaugh family; Paradise Wildlife Park, Broxbourne www.pwpark.com.